Old Wars Remain Unfinished

OLD WARS REMAIN UNFINISHED

The Veteran Benefits System

SAR A. LEVITAN
KAREN A. CLEARY

THE JOHNS HOPKINS UNIVERSITY PRESS
BALTIMORE AND LONDON

This book was prepared under a grant from the Ford Foundation.

The photographs in this book are reprinted by courtesy of
the Veterans Administration.

The charts were prepared by "The Hatchet."

The Johns Hopkins University Press, Baltimore, Maryland 21218
The Johns Hopkins University Press Ltd., London

Library of Congress Catalog Card Number 73–8117
ISBN 0–8018–1515–0

Library of Congress Cataloging in Publication data
will be found on the last printed page of this book.

Remember that old wars remain unfinished,
That men fail, fall, and are replenished.

HORACE GREGORY
"Voices of Heroes"

Contents

Preface

Since the beginning of this nation, the federal government has maintained an income support program for war veterans. Over the years, programs in aid of veterans have evolved into a comprehensive welfare system.

Until the emergence of the New Deal legislation, the federal assistance to veterans was unique because all other governmental welfare responsibilities were left to state and local governments. But the New Deal and the Great Society have not only expanded federal responsibility, but also induced state and local government to establish for the rest of the population assistance that was available traditionally only to veterans. Medicaid has made health care available to the indigent and near poor population, Medicare provided the same to most aged persons, and income support to the poor has become widespread though not universal. Education and training programs for veterans also have their counterparts for nonveterans.

Nonetheless, the separate veterans' programs are sustained and their persistence is not due to inertia alone. The welfare standards in effect for veterans are much more liberal than for nonveterans, and the rules of the game are also different. Though the means test controls both veterans' and nonveterans' programs, the veterans' program operates with due regard for the dignity of the individual, while the recipients of welfare aid are held in opprobium.

It might be surprising to an outsider, therefore, that the veterans' system of which we could be justly proud receives so little attention, while the other welfare system has been at the center of public discussion and has become a major domestic political issue in recent years. The veterans' welfare system shows that a means-tested program does not have to be mean and that we are capable of developing a reasonable system to help a selected sector of the needy population. The present debate about overhauling the welfare system for the rest of the population presents a challenge to do for the total population what we have done for veterans.

Many taxpayers view welfare as a four-letter word, and some will object to identifying aid to veterans as a welfare system. However, concern for the welfare of the people is in line with the democratic tradition. Indeed, the Constitution coupled "common Defense and general Welfare of the United States" as a major responsibility of Congress.

This volume examines the programs in aid of veterans. A brief historical treatment describing how the veterans' system has evolved is accompanied by an analysis of the institutions which are involved in veterans' programs. These include the Veterans Administration and other federal agencies that serve veterans, the "processing" of veteran legislation in Congress, and the role that the several veterans' organizations play in furthering veterans' causes on Capitol Hill.

Separate chapters are devoted to income support, health delivery, and the education and training offered to veterans. The law distinguishes between two groups of veterans. Special consideration is given to the veteran who was injured in the performance of his duties while in the armed forces. The disabled veteran is entitled to income support for the rest of his life, and the level of support is determined by the extent of his injury. The government also provides health care to the disabled veteran, and special consideration and rehabilitation to aid his readjustment to civilian life.

Other veterans are entitled to income support or medical assistance only in case of need, but need is liberally interpreted. Income of veterans can be considerably higher than the cutoff levels for public assistance or Medicaid eligibility for other near-poor. The system has virtually eliminated poverty, as defined by government criteria, among the incapacitated and aged veteran population, and their surviving dependents.

The government also offers special assistance to former servicemen upon their discharge from the military duty to help them adjust to civilian life. Nearly three decades have elapsed since the original GI bill of rights was passed in preparation for the end of hostilities during World War II. Millions of veterans owe their college education or vocational training to the special aid offered by the government. But the assistance offered to Vietnam veterans has been less generous than the aid offered to World War II veterans.

Altogether, the federal government spends about $12 billion a year in aid of veterans. The outlays have been growing rapidly, as have all other welfare expenditures. As the welfare system for the rest of the population expands and becomes increasingly generous, the question is whether a separate welfare system for veterans will be needed and whether it should be sustained. If past experience is any guide to the future, it can be expected that the advocates and administrators of the veterans' programs will succeed in keeping the aid offered a step, or two ahead of what is provided for the rest of the population, and thus offer sufficient incentives to an influential clientele to demand the continuation of the special assistance offered. As long as the United States continues to get involved in wars, there will be a constituency that will insist that veterans' programs are to continue.

I am grateful to William Johnston for his critical and insightful review of the draft, to Joyce Zickler for her research assistance on chapter 4, and to Barbara Pease for her help in preparing the manuscript. Officials of the Veterans Administration and the Department of Labor were most generous with their time and cooperation in making available the data upon which this volume is based.

This volume was prepared under a grant from The Ford Foundation to The George Washington University's Center for Manpower Policy Studies. In accordance with the foundation's practice, complete responsibility for the preparation of the volume has been left to the authors.

Veterans Day, 1972   SAR A. LEVITAN

Old Wars Remain Unfinished

CHAPTER 1

The Veterans' Welfare System

These are the times that try men's souls.
The summer soldier and the sunshine patriot will,
in this crisis, shrink from the service of his country;
but he that stands it NOW, deserves the love and thanks
of man and woman.

Thomas Paine
The American Crisis, No. 1, December 19, 1776

The United States government supports a dual welfare system. One applies to the general population, couched in the tradition of the Elizabethan Poor Law, mandating state and local jurisdictions to maintain their destitute. The second is exclusively for the veteran population, and has evolved from a tradition of compensating former servicemen damaged in the course of their military duty. The existence of special benefits for veterans is not a unique American institution; most developed nations maintain special benefits for exservicemen and their families, especially for those who have been killed or maimed in service.

In 1972 the United States government spent $11.5 billion on behalf of veterans. These expenditures cover an intricate welfare system ranging from helping young veterans find jobs or learn a skill to the payment of burial expenditures for deceased veterans. The major outlays included support to compensate veterans injured in the service of their country, pensions for indigent and incapacitated veterans and their surviving dependents, health care, education and training, and unemployment benefits for recently separated veterans who could not find employment (chart 1).

By the time the United States celebrates its second hundredth anniversary it will have spent over $250 billion for the care and support of its war veterans. World War II accounted for nearly half of these outlays, and if past experience is any indication, most of the costs of support of World War II veterans is still ahead of us and will dwarf outlays for veterans of earlier and more recent wars. Expenditures for Korean Conflict veterans have already surpassed support for veterans through the Spanish-American War, and outlays for Vietnam veterans even before the war was terminated exceeded more than 70 years expenditures for Spanish-American veterans (table 1).

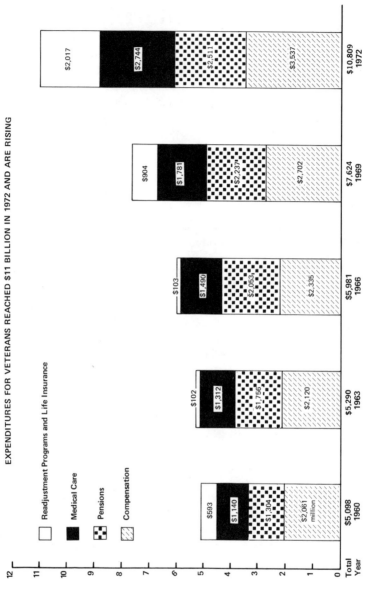

CHART 1

EXPENDITURES FOR VETERANS REACHED $11 BILLION IN 1972 AND ARE RISING

Source: Veterans Administration and the Department of Labor.

Table 1. Outlays for Veterans' Programs through June 30, 1972

(millions)

Outlay	All Wars	Vietnam Era	Korean Conflict	World War II	World War I	Spanish-American War	Other Wars and Regular Establishment
Total	$195,838	$7,271	$16,960	$96,447	$52,411	$5,526	$17,223
Cash Benefits	154,480	6,212	11,913	74,536	41,770	5,072	14,967
Bonus	3,820	—	—	—	3,820	—	—
Compensation and Pensions—Total	106,221	1,574	5,852	46,226	35,019	5,044	12,506
Compensation	—	1,546	5,122	38,269	11,893	—	—
Veterans	—	1,199	4,082	30,931	9,319	—	—
Dependents	—	374	1,030	7,338	2,574	—	—
Pensions	—	28	740	7,958	23,126	—	—
Veterans	—	13	307	4,358	16,349	—	—
Dependents	—	15	433	3,599	6,777	—	—
Insurance and indemnities	6,653	35	391	4,781	1,429	—	18
Vocational rehabilitation and training	2,723	147	198	1,635	645	—	97
Education and training	25,076	3,905	4,596	14,837	—	—	1,721
Readjustment allowance	3,805	—	—	3,805	—	—	—
Loan guaranty	4,595	508	818	2,666	—	—	602
Autos, invalid lifts & special devices	124	23	6	84	5	—	6
Homes for paraplegics	123	12	14	74	11	—	12
Burial allowances	1,003	8	38	426	488	29	14
Military and naval family allowance	282	—	—	—	282	—	—
Health care	32,451	816	4,125	16,071	9,151	398	1,888
Capital additions and improvements	2,093	26	216	1,621	195	9	26
Administrative costs	6,815	217	706	4,219	1,295	47	331

Source: Veterans Administration.

The costs of veterans' programs have been mounting steadily as a result of expanding benefits, rising costs of medical care, and an increasing veteran population. But their proportion of total federal outlays has remained rather stable during recent years because other federal nondefense expenditures have been rising at unprecedented rates. In the seven years following the advent of the Great Society, total federal outlays for income support, health, education, and training—the major areas of veterans' programs—have nearly tripled while veteran benefits doubled (chart 2).

Veteran Population

As of 1971, one of every seven Americans was a veteran and, together with their dependents, about half of the U.S. population were potential beneficiaries of veterans' programs. Veterans range in age from teenagers to old men pushing past the century mark. In 1970, 43.6 percent of all males aged 18 and over had experienced military service and 90 percent of them were war veterans. While veterans come in all ages, the largest concentration of veterans in the 1970s is among the middle-aged male population, reflecting the maturation of the 14.3 million World War II veterans whose average age in 1971 was 52 years (chart 3). By 1971 two million veterans had reached the traditional retirement age of 65 and over. Most of these (1.4 million) were survivors of World War I, with an average age of 77, but an additional 581,000 senior veterans were from World War II. These are the vanguards of the aging World War II population. As World War II veteran age, the numbers of retired veterans will multiply. By 1995 the veteran population over 65 will quadruple. Since the bulk of veteran expenditures is for income maintenance and health care programs, outlays for World War II veterans will rise as their physical infirmities increase and age reduces their earning power.

Racial Composition

Blacks and other racial minority groups are underrepresented in the veteran population. While 10.7 percent of American males 16 years and older are non-Caucasion, blacks and other non-Caucasians constitute only 7.7 percent of veteran population. The statistics reflect past and persisting discriminatory practices. Prior to 1948, discrimination was official and the armed forces segregated Negro and other minority groups and relegated them to menial positions. Moreover, deficiencies in health and education also contributed to the underrepresentation of blacks in the armed services. Their inability to

CHART 2

FEDERAL BUDGET OUTLAYS FOR HUMAN RESOURCES HAVE NEARLY
TRIPLED BETWEEN 1965 AND 1972

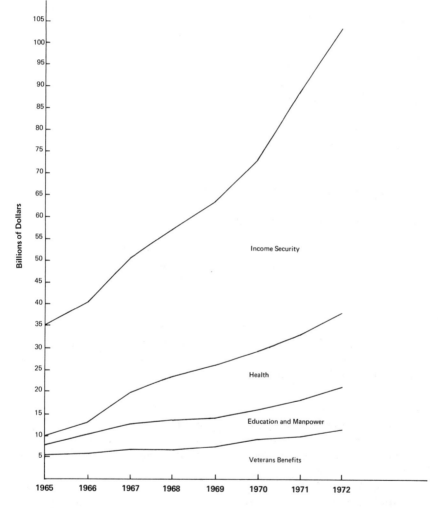

Source: U.S. Bureau of the Census, *Statistical Abstract of the United States,*
1972 (Washington: Government Printing Office, 1972), p. 386.

qualify on physical, mental, and trainability tests remained a problem
for minority groups even after the elimination of outright segregation.
Only 8.8 percent of Vietnam era veterans were members of minority
races. The percent of blacks serving in the armed services had in-

CHART 3

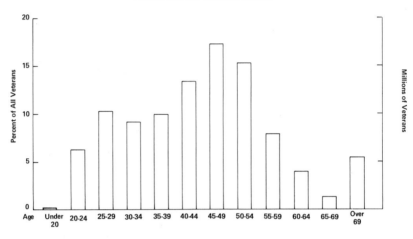

VETERANS COME IN ALL AGES BUT THE MAJORITY ARE
MIDDLE AGED WORLD WAR II VINTAGE

Source: Veterans Administration, 1972.

creased to 9.9 percent in 1971, but still remained below their percentage in the population.

Education and Income

Veterans as a group are better educated and more affluent than their nonveteran counterparts. Veterans have attained a median educational level of 12.5 years schooling, compared with the 12.1 years attained by male nonveterans; this reflects the military's selection processes. The income differential is even greater. The veteran's median income in 1970 was $8,660, surpassing the median income of nonveteran adult males by $2,800. The median family income of war veterans—82 percent of whom were family heads—was $12,020, compared to $9,150 median income of families headed by nonveteran males.

The 2.1 million veterans who, according to the Bureau of the Census, were "unrelated individuals," that is lived alone and not as part of a family, had a median income of $5,627 in 1970. Older veterans aged 65 and over are overrepresented in this group, and their average annual income of $2,661 tends to pull down the income of the "unrelated individuals." However, the income of these aged veterans still exceeded by $657 the median income of "unrelated" aged nonveterans. The income support programs for veterans contributed to this income differential.

Overview of Veterans' Benefits

Special provision for veterans, especially service-disabled soldiers, date back even before the Revolution to the wars of the early settlers against the Indians and the French. The earliest recorded veterans' statute, a Plymouth Colony law of 1636, provided:

> In case necessity require to send forces abroad, and there be not volunteers sufficient offered for the service, then be it lawful for the Governor and [his] assistants to presse [men into service] in his Majesties name ... provided that if any that shall goe returne mamed & hurt, he shall be maytayned competently by the colony duringe his life.[1]

Revolutionary war soldiers were promised service pensions in order to keep morale up and desertions down. A commission, appointed by the Continental Congress, recommended in 1776 "half-pay for life, or during disability, to every officer, soldier, or sailor losing a limb in battle" or who was incapacitated and could no longer earn a living. Those partially disabled were to be given proportionate relief. The states were to finance the disability pension plan.[2] A second measure passed in 1778 promised officers half pay for 7 years and enlisted personnel were promised mustering-out pay of $80 if they served until the end of the war. In addition to monetary rewards, Revolutionary War soldiers were offered land grants as enticement to serve and remain in the army. Grants ranged from 100 acres for a private to 1,100 for a major general.

Since the Continental Congress had little authority over the "several states," and remained without resources to carry out its obligations, the execution of the laws varied from state to state. The southern states tended to honor the obligation to pay pensions and northern states reneged, finding ideological justifications for the action. To some, the special treatment afforded officers constituted favoritism not compatible with the ideals of the new republic. Furthermore, many certificates testifying to the officers' claims for pensions had fallen into the hands of speculators.

The payment of the federal debt, including veterans' pensions, became a point of contention between northern and southern states that held up ratification of the constitution. A compromise worked out by Thomas Jefferson and Alexander Hamilton resolved the issue, the capitol of the new constitutional government was to be located in the South between Virginia and Maryland instead of in a northern city, in exchange for southern support of national debt assumption, including pensions.[3] Following the agreement, the federal Congress took over payment of pensions from the states and the veterans' programs have been an integral part of the federal budget since the birth of the nation. In the words of Veterans Administration historian Robinson E. Adkins, the federal Congress became "the guardian of the disabled veteran, his widow, and his orphan—a right which it has jealously guarded ever since."[4]

Early federal activities on behalf of veterans consisted of minor readjustment benefits that singled out officers. Benefits of land grants, mustering-out pay and half pay to officers acted more as an inducement to keep soldiers in service than to help their readjustment to civil life. The initial law providing compensation to men injured in service pinpointed the most basic responsibility of the government toward its fighting men. As the Revolutionary War veteran population aged and the U.S. Treasury grew, pressure mounted to extend pensions to all Revolutionary War veterans, especially those in poverty. The first general veterans' pension enacted in 1818 based eligibility on "need," paying out $20 a month to former officers and $8 a month to enlisted personnel. The "needs" test was removed a decade later, qualifying all surviving Revolutionary War officers to their full military pay for life instead of the half pay promised in 1780. In 1832, the same benefits were extended to all Revolutionary War veterans who served at least two years, and pension amounts were prorated by length of service if the veteran served less than two years. However, the means test that was dropped in 1832 was revived for veterans of later wars.

General pensions for widows were first established in 1836. The law provided that any widow of a Revolutionary War veteran who would have been eligible for a service pension under the 1832 act could collect the pension in his stead. Early provisions for widows contained no income conditions since few had independent income, and most widows were dependent on fathers, sons, or other relations for support. When the husband died, the widow was considered in need. Pensions terminated upon remarriage. Later laws incorporated income limitations for widows.

Provision of special facilities for aged and disabled veterans was the next step. The earliest endeavor was the establishment in 1833 of U.S. Naval Home for decrepit or disabled personnel. It was financed by deductions from the pay of seamen. In 1851, a U.S. Soldiers' Home opened in Washington, D.C. for disabled former soldiers.

Until the Civil War, the United States could well afford to take care of its veterans because their numbers were small and other demands on the U.S. Treasury were few. Of the 290,000 participants in the Revolutionary War, 286,000 survived, making up about 7 percent of the total 1790 population. The period between the Revolutionary War and the Civil War was disturbed only by two rather confined wars involving a total of 366,000 fighting men. The War of 1812 left 285,000 veterans and the Mexican War, which ended in 1848, left

86,000 veterans. Thus veterans as a group represented a shrinking proportion of the rapidly expanding U.S. population. Altogether, there were approximately 80,000 veterans at the outbreak of the Civil War.

By 1865, the Civil War had added nearly another 1.9 million veterans. These were only from the Union army. Confederate veterans did not receive any veteran benefits from the federal government until 1958, when Congress formally pardoned Confederate forces and made pensions available to the few survivors. This large veteran population generated greater demand for veteran programs, resulting in the expansion of institutional facilities to provide for the disabled. The National Asylums for Disabled Soldiers—later named National Homes—were established in 1866 to provide residential facilities for Union soldiers. Southern states assumed a similar responsibility for Confederate soldiers, who were barred from the National Homes.

The 1.9 million Union veterans constituted a significant minority in the population, and had considerable political clout. Though the number of veterans continued to decline during the next two generations until the end of World War I, annual expenditures for veterans continued to climb, with only brief halts. In the five years following the Civil War, the United States expended more funds in behalf of veterans than during the preceding eighty years. The post-Civil War period marked the beginning of widespread special institutions for the care of veterans. National Homes emphasized the provision of residential facilities, but the incidental medical care they provided domiciled residents expanded into an integral part of the organized hospital system. Apparently believing that those who were asked to serve their nation in time of stress would also be encouraged to serve under more propitious conditions, veterans were extended preference in public employment.

The half century following the Civil war was relatively peaceful. The major crusade during this period, the Spanish-American War, was a skirmish compared with the bloody Civil War and World War I. The Indian wars, with the exception of Little Big Horn and a few other incidents, were mostly police actions if not masacres of Indians.

World War I added 4.7 million veterans. Among those who fought in the war there were 204,000 wounded and 116,000 killed. The large veteran population gave rise to new veteran programs. War Risk Insurance, originally designed to protect cargoes, came to represent a major veterans' benefit for doughboys as servicemen bought insurance against death and permanent disability. A hospital system for veterans evolved out of the Public Health Service hospitals. In addition, organized rehabilitation programs were offered to disabled veterans, although compensation payments were low.

World War I veterans returned to civilian life when the economy was sagging, and the government made few provisions to aid their readjustment. The bulk of the veterans were, of course, not eligible for diability compensation, and many could not find employment. The result was considerable discontent. When programs for World War II veterans were being designed, the spectre of World War I veterans peddling apples on street corners and marching on Washington for a service "bonus" weighed heavily in the planners' consideration. For this and a number of other reasons, the nation's responsibility to its veterans was thought of in much wider terms after the Second World War.

First, tremendous numbers of veterans were affected, over 16 million by the end of the war, and there was concern about the impact of a massive troop demobilization. In late 1945 and early 1946, one million veterans a month were reentering the civilian society. At the same time, a quick and steady transition was being made from a defense-based to a peacetime economy. Memories of the mass unemployment of the Great Depression were still fresh, and fear was rampant that joblessness would skyrocket, leaving millions of bitter veterans wandering the streets. Congress was anxious to avoid a second "bonus" battle and provided for smoother transition to civilian life.

A second reason for assuming a new responsibility was the duration of service for many of the veterans. This had not been a brief interruption; United States active participation in the shooting war lasted nearly four years, and millions served for the duration of the war. 671,000 were wounded in the Second World War, and there were survivors of 406,000 who had been killed; the greater numbers increased the seriousness of the responsibility.

A third reason for assuming greater responsibility was the growing conviction that there was an educational deficit among the young men of the nation and that the maintenance of newly acquired world leadership depended upon broadening the base of scientific and technological attainment in the country.

Finally, it was believed that the nation owed a debt of gratitude to veterans for their service. "War sacrifices," declared the prestigious presidential commission on veterans' programs headed by General Omar Bradley, "should be distributed as equally as possible within our society."[5] Possibly no less relevant were the persisting memories of maimed World War I veterans without any means of support; and the nation attempted to avoid the chaos that might result from much larger numbers returning from World War II.

All these factors led to a drastic redefinition of the nation's responsibilities to veterans. Not only would the nation contribute to the initial readjustment of all veterans through a variety of efforts; its responsibility was extended to help make up for the time lost in service and to replace lost opportunities with new ones. The veteran was entitled to an opportunity to "catch up" with the nonveterans who remained behind.

For these reasons, Congress enacted a comprehensive set of programs to help the returning veterans to adjust to civilian life. The newly enacted law, popularly known as the GI bill of rights, assumed that the readjustment difficulties faced by the veterans would be widespread. The provisions for assisting all veterans—not just injured servicemen—can be conveniently classified into three major categories: education and training, employment assistance, and housing.

Benefits to enable the veteran to continue his education, supplement it with training, or to begin a new direction of education or training were designed to assist the veteran to compete more adequately with the nonveterans who did not serve and to compensate for opportunities lost because of military service. Although different types of education and training were involved, the benefit originally took the form of a subsistence allowance coupled with a tuition grant paid directly to the school.

For veterans who desired jobs, there were also a variety of programs and benefits to facilitate the transition from military to civilian employment. Assistance in the form of unemployment benefits, counseling and guidance, placement, or opportunities for special preference in employment were legislated. Although this type of assistance was generally available to all unemployed, special emphasis in these programs was placed on assisting returning veterans.

The third effort on behalf of veterans' guaranteed loans to enable them to purchase housing—the GI Guaranty Loan Program. Direct loans were also authorized in areas where commercial guaranteed loans were unavailable to veterans to purchase a house. Grants to severely disabled veterans for specially adapted housing were also made available.

The comprehensive World War II GI bill served as a basis for assisting veterans readjustment in the next two United States wars during the succeeding generation. Though never officially declared as "wars," the Korean Conflict and the Vietnam War added another 9.6 million veterans eligible to receive benefits. The readjustment program gained widespread support and it was revived following the Korean Conflict, even though most veterans had spent a shorter period in the service than World War II veterans. The prevailing opinion was that Korean veterans should be treated equally with their World War II counterparts. Feeble attempts were made to continue the readjustment opportunities of education and training for the veterans of peacetime service after Korea, but there was little support for the notion. Even the major veterans' organizations opposed the move on the basis that the nation did not have the same responsibility to a peacetime veteran as it did to a war veteran. The interruption caused by a peacetime draft was not felt to engender either the same physical and mental hardships, nor as difficult readjustment problems as service during a war period.

As the fighting in Vietnam progressed and both death toll and numbers returning from that war increased, service organizations pressed for extension of benefits to Vietnam veterans similar to those extended to veterans of the two preceeding wars. Later these opportunities were also retroactively offered to the 3.1 million veterans who served during the "cold war" era prior to the escalation of war in Vietnam.

Program Administration

Until the Veterans Administration was established in 1930 to administer most veterans' programs, assistance was handled by several agencies. The Department of the Interior paid pensions, National Homes for Disabled Volunteer Soldiers were administered by a semi-autonomous agency in the Interior Department, and the Public Health Service was responsible for the administration of hospitals caring for veterans. The Treasury Department administered War Risk Insurance, which provided death and injury compensation. In 1921, Congress consolidated these services by establishing the Veterans Bureau, which absorbed the Public Health Service functions and the War Risk Insurance. Nine years later, the Veterans Administration replaced the bureau, and the jurisdiction of the new agency was expanded to include the Bureau of Pensions and National Homes.

The operational functions of the VA are divided into three major departments. The Department of Medicine and Surgery has jurisdiction over all medical care and related activities; the Department of Veterans Benefits operates all financial assistance programs; and the Department of Data Management churns out the usual housekeeping data and analysis of agency activities (figure 1).

The movement, favored by the Johnson and Nixon administrations, to decentralize the operation of domestic departments and agencies has not affected the Veterans Administration. Instead of the usual ten regional offices common to other domestic agencies, the VA has divided the country into four areas with regional directors to monitor the field operations. The directors are located in the Washington office of the Veterans Administration and report to the chief medical officer and to the head of the Department of Veterans Benefits.

FIGURE 1

ORGANIZATION OF THE VETERANS ADMINISTRATION

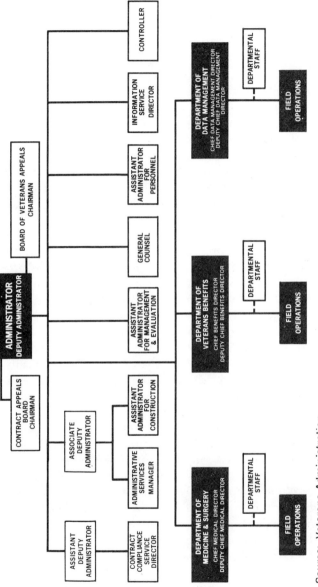

Source: Veterans Administration.

The real work of the VA—the servicing of veterans—has always been decentralized. Fifty-seven regional offices and the medical field stations which include 167 hospitals, 18 domiciliaries, and other related facilities offer widely disbursed services to veterans (figure 2). All the field station directors report to Washington; the medical field stations to the regional medical directors, and the regional officers to the area field directors. This highly decentralized operation was interupted for a short period after World War II, between 1946 and 1949, when 13 branch offices were established with considerable authority over the operations of the field stations. But the established regional officials apparently resented the intrusion of middle-level authority between the operating units and the policy makers in Washington, and they succeeded in eliminating the interlopers. The official reason for doing away with the regional offices, or branch offices as they were known in the VA, was to avoid overlapping responsibility. Field offices were then placed in the central office in Washington.[6]

The organization of the Washington office is similar to that of other large federal agencies. Most of the staff positions are common to federal agencies, although a few are tailored specifically to the mission of the VA. Possibly the most significant among the latter is the Board of Veterans Appeals, which has final jurisdiction over the granting or denial of benefits. Other federal agencies also have internal adjudicating systems, and the internal veterans' appeals system is, therefore, not unique. In the case of veterans' benefits, however, Congress had legislated that no other court may review the decisions of the administrator that pertain to veterans' benefits, and a 1970 law firmly reiterated the administrator's exclusive right to review appeals. The rationale for this unusual arrangement is that veterans' benefits are gratuities, and Congress has the right to foreclose judicial review of such benefits.[7]

In 1972, the Veterans Administration employed 172,000 persons full time, a staff second in size only to that of the Defense Department. However, most VA employees are assigned to the operation of hospitals, with only 24,000 employed in delivery of nonmedical services.

While almost all veterans' monetary benefits and most of the other services are administered by the VA, other federal agencies, state government organizations, and private veterans' organizations play a role in dispensing services to veterans. The Department of Health, Education and Welfare and the Department of Labor are involved in the education, training, and job placement of veterans, and the Labor Department administers the payment of unemployment benefits. The Department of Defense has also expanded its responsibility for servicemen to include aid for their transition to civilian life and has its own information, counseling, and training programs.

Veterans' Organizations

It is natural that veterans with a common patriotic experience and with a considerable direct interest in public policy would band together to form their own organizations for fellowship and to protect and further their own interests. The Grand Army of the Republic, organized in 1865, was the first major national veterans' organization. While the rhetoric of the Grand Army of the Republic (GAR) tended to stress fraternal and patriotic goals, the GAR was not adverse to partisan politics. GAR, one observer suggested, connoted "generally all Republican" and its detractors charged that the GAR's paramount interest was raiding the treasury, rather than advancing the more lofty objectives it professed.[8]

Present-day veterans' organizations somewhat resemble their illustrious predecessor. While the GAR was necessarily a regional organization limited to Union veterans, current veteran organizations are national in scope. Otherwise, the current organizations share with the GAR the dual role of purely social organizations and self-seeking lobbies for veterans' benefits. The veterans' organizations received their charters from Congress, which specified their objectives to be fraternal, patriotic, and educational. The organizations perpetuate the memory of dead veterans, dedicate themselves to preserve and defend the United States from all her enemies, and offer assistance to their members and the widows and orphans of exservicemen. Unlike the GAR, the modern-day veteran organizations have officially shunned partisan politics and have focused their activities on patriotic causes and issues that pertain directly to veterans. The extent to which the activities of these organizations are centered on bread and butter issues rather than civic causes depends a great deal upon who the observer is.

Membership and Goals

The five major veterans' organizations are the American Legion, Veterans of Foreign Wars, Disabled American Veterans, AMVETS, and Veterans of World War I of the United States, Inc. These organizations claimed the following membership in 1972:

American Legion—2.7 million
Veterans of Foreign Wars—1.7 million
Disabled American Veterans—340,000
AMVETS—250,000
Veterans of World War I of the United States, Inc.—220,000.

There are a number of smaller veterans' groups that tend to be either religious or ethnic in origin or one-issue organizations. Jewish

FIGURE 2

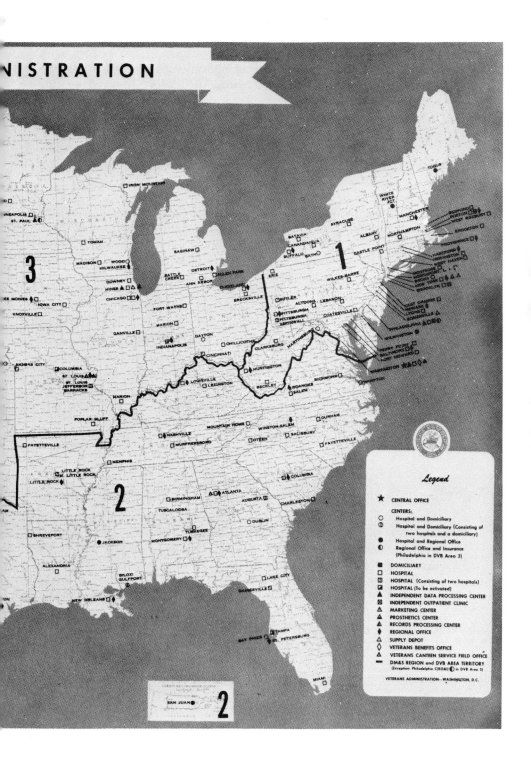

3

1

2

IRON MOUNTAIN

NEAPOLIS
ST. PAUL

TOMAH

MADISON   WOOD
MILWAUKEE
DOWNEY
HINES   CHICAGO

SAGINAW

BATTLE
CREEK   DETROIT
ALLEN PARK
ANN ARBOR
CLEVELAND

ES MOINES
IOWA CITY
KNOXVILLE

FORT WAYNE

MARION

DANVILLE   INDIANAPOLIS
DAYTON

BRECKSVILLE

BUTLER
PITTSBURGH
ASPINWALL

ALTOONA   LEBANON
COATESVILLE

CHILLICOTHE

CINCINNATI   CLARKSBURG   MARTIN

KANSAS CITY
COLUMBIA
ST. LOUIS
JEFFERSON
BARRACKS
MARION

LOUISVILLE   LEXINGTON

HUNTINGTON

BECKLEY   ROANOKE
SALEM   RICHMOND

POPLAR BLUFF

FAYETTEVILLE

MOUNTAIN HOME   WINSTON-SALEM
OTEEN   SALISBURY   DURHAM
NASHVILLE   FAYETTEVILLE
MURFREESBORO

MEMPHIS

LITTLE ROCK
N. LITTLE ROCK
LITTLE ROCK

COLUMBIA

BIRMINGHAM   ATLANTA
AUGUSTA   CHARLESTON

SHREVEPORT

TUSCALOOSA

DUBLIN

JACKSON   MONTGOMERY   TUSKEGEE

ALEXANDRIA

BILOXI
GULFPORT   LAKE CITY
GAINESVILLE

NEW ORLEANS

BAY PINES   TAMPA
ST. PETERSBURG

MIAMI

TOGUS

WHITE
RIVER
JCT.

MANCHESTER   NORTHAMPTON

REDDING
BOSTON
WEST ROXBURY
BROCKTON

SYRACUSE   ALBANY

BATAVIA
CANANDAIGUA
BUFFALO   BATH

CASTLE POINT

WILKES-BARRE

ERIE

HASTINGS
WASHINGTON
WEST HAVEN

BRONX
NEW YORK
BROOKLYN

EAST ORANGE
LYONS

PHILADELPHIA

WILMINGTON

PERRY POINT
BALTIMORE
FORT HOWARD

HAMPTON

WASHINGTON

SAN JUAN   **2**

War Veterans and Catholic War Veterans are examples of the former. Veterans of World War I of the United States, Inc., have focused their attention primarily on a general service pension for World War I veterans. The National Association of Collegiate Veterans, formed in 1968, concentrates on liberalizing educational benefits; while the Paralyzed American Veterans are concerned with improved benefits and better medical care for veterans with spinal cord injuries. The American Veterans Committee supports liberalized readjustment benefits for veterans, but tends to emphasize civil rights rather than veterans' rights. The above list is by no means exhaustive; there are many more organizations allegedly representing veterans, but most of these are neither chartered by Congress nor recognized by the Veterans Administration as service organizations.

The total membership of veterans' organizations is between 5 and 6 million. Ignoring duplication of membership, this would mean that about every fifth veteran is a member of a veterans' organization. Since dues tend to be low—average annual dues at the American Legion and the Veterans of Foreign Wars are $7.00—it would not be surprising if there is considerable duplication of membership. The largest organization, the American Legion, accepts all honorably discharged veterans who have served in a period of hostility. The Veterans of Foreign Wars is limited to war veterans who have served in a war zone. Eligibility for the Disabled American Veterans is limited to veterans who have suffered a service-connected disability. It would thus appear that most DAV members are also eligible for membership in VFW and all of them are eligible for membership in the American Legion. The Legion is reported to have estimated that 10 to 12 percent of its members also belong to other veterans' organizations.[9]

Whether the power of veterans' organizations is waning remains a matter of debate. It is clear, however, that their membership has declined from a post-World War II peak, although the number of veterans has increased. The American Legion's membership in 1946 was 3.3 million; a generation later, with some 10 million more veterans to draw from, the membership had declined to a reported 2.7 million in 1970. According to one report the major veterans' organizations are barely holding on to their old membership and relatively few of the more recent veterans have joined their ranks.[10] The American Legion denied this allegation, claiming that new recruits have more than replaced resignations and deaths, resulting in a 150,000 membership boost since 1964. The Legion claimed 325,000 members who served in Vietnam, but did not support the claim with hard data.[11]

While veterans' organizations shun partisan politics, they generally tend to take conservative positions on political issues. Given their predominantly middle-aged, middle-class constituency, the veterans' organizations are likely to be found on the side of the establishment. The confrontations between the veterans' organizations and the government that followed World War I and continued into the depression of the 1930s were not repeated after World War II. Any serious liberalization of veterans' benefits would run into billions of dollars, and such financial extravagance is not likely to get support from the veterans' organizations. The American Legion and the Veterans of Foreign Wars have accordingly settled on a more passive role in influencing veterans' legislation by following what the majority of Congress, many of whom are also veterans, has been willing to grant to veterans. The leadership for this live-and-let-live arrangement has been provided by Congressman Olin E. Teague, a conservative Democrat and a Legion member from Texas, who chaired the Veterans Affairs Committee in the House between 1955 and 1973, and by his successor William Jennings Bryan Dorn.

It is, however, misleading to speak of veterans' organizations as if they spoke with one voice. Disparity of goals and rivalry among these organizations impedes cooperation on legislative programs to some degree. Each of the major veterans' organizations marches up to Capitol Hill with its own set of programs, but except for lip-service, Congress pays little attention to their proposals. It is evident that the two major veterans' organizations have no inclination to rock the boat. On the contrary, veterans may be getting less than they could actually demand and get from Congress. For example, under the education and training program, the area of major expansion during the 1960s, payments to veterans were less generous than after World War II. Since the trend in other welfare programs has been to at least maintain earlier levels and to expand programs, it might be argued that veterans' organizations have failed the Vietnam veterans either because of waning political clout or because they are content with the present system. Reflecting on the aging of their membership, one critical observer of the veterans' organizations charged that their lobbyists have shown greater interest in burial benefits than in educational programs.

The American Legion and the Veterans of Foreign Wars are largely local civic and patriotic clubs and play only a minor role on the national scene. Given their present constituency and their age mix, it would not be realistic to expect these organizations to act otherwise. It would require a major social upheaval or a radical change in membership for the veterans' organizations to make more militant demands on behalf of their constituency.

The American Legion and the other veterans' organizations have, on the other hand, maintained cordial relations with the Veterans Administration. Appointments to high posts in the Veterans Administration are often given to men who have held top leadership positions in veterans' organizations. The director of Veterans Administration since 1969, Donald E. Johnson, was a past national commander of the American Legion and its general counsel, John J. Corcoran, was formerly a top official in the American Legion bureaucracy. Other government posts outside the VA have been filled with former veterans' group leaders; for instance, the present head of the Veteran Employment Service is the former VFW commander, Herbert R. Rainwater.

The American Veterans Committee deviates markedly from its sister organizations, and other veterans' groups will not even recognize it as part of the same family. The AVC agrees with the other organizations on compensating service-generated needs, but is opposed to all other special programs for veterans. For example, while the other veterans' organizations favor nonservice-connected pensions, presumably because they believe that the payments prevent the veteran from becoming an object of "public charity" and entitle him to support with dignity, the AVC is opposed to "special grants or favors to veterans."[12] The AVC considers benefits other than service-connected compensation and readjustment as "class legislation." The AVC has had, however, little appeal to veterans; even if its claims of 80,000 members were true, it would still account for only 1 percent of the total veterans who have joined service organizations.

Lobby Activities

Veterans' organizations live in the best of all possible worlds as lobby groups. Their status as "patriotic organizations" is a matter of law and is spelled out in Title 36 of the U.S. Code, an enviable position for any special interest group. Recognized primarily as civic service organizations, the veterans' organizations are not only tax exempt but are supported in many other ways by tax dollars. For instance, office space for organization service officers is provided in VA hospitals and contact centers. The annual proceedings of the conventions are printed as congressional documents, and policy resolutions which require legislative action invariably find their way to the *Congressional Record*.

Access to Congress and other top political officials is no problem for patriotic organizations with membership running into hundreds of thousands or millions and with access to news media and their own publications. The *American Legion Magazine* is a monthly publication with a circulation of about 2.7 million and the Veterans for Foreign Wars publish the monthly *V*F*W Magazine*. In addition, the American Legion publishes two other monthly mass circulation magazines:

The Firing Line, devoted to patriotic causes, and *Speaking of Children,* focusing on problems of juvenile delinquency, drug abuse, and related child and youth problems. In addition, a bimonthly legislative bulletin focuses on issues involving veterans' benefits. The other veterans' organizations have similar publications. Over half the legislators are themselves members of one or more veterans' groups and receive their information first hand.

Each major veterans' organization maintains legislative offices in Washington. The professional staff in these offices not only act as lobbyists for veterans' programs but also for causes not directly related to veterans' benefits. They do what comes naturally to Washington lobbyists, chanking out information about their favorite programs and serving sympathizers in Congress and in the executive offices.

Lobbyists for the veterans' organizations operate in a friendly atmosphere. While there is considerable rivalry among the organizations for bodies, there is little struggle over the souls of potential members. The lobbyists as professionals with common aims and similar ideologies cooperate in getting their objectives across, but carefully avoid asking for too much and thereby alienating otherwise conservative members of Congress. The challenge, as one of the top veterans' lobbyists observed, is to keep the programs "within limits acceptable to the taxpayers." Indeed, it is highly doubtful whether the membership of the American Legion and the Veterans of Foreign Wars would tolerate excessive demands upon the Treasury. The task of the lobbyists and their friends in Congress is to select top priority objectives that will muster sufficient congressional and public support, and therefore will be accepted by Congress and the administration. The selection of "an idea whose time has come," according to a Veterans Administration spokesman, is the collective task of the veterans' lobbying community. Being an essentially conservative lot, the inclination is not to press new and novel ideas or controversial legislation. For instance, proposals to open VA hospitals to children and wives of men who were totally disabled or died as the result of military service has been viewed by veterans' organizations as promotion of empty promises. The task of the lobbyist, therefore, is not only to help create the pressure for the idea and to shepherd it through the legislative process, but also to select the right priorities.

Aside from selecting substantive issues for legislation, the veterans' legislative representatives are also concerned that all programs on behalf of veterans be centrally administered by the Veterans Administration. Francis Stover, VFW's legislative director, claimed that "the veterans' preference gets lost in any program for veterans unless it is administered by the Veterans Administration."[13] With the expansion of federally-supported social and welfare legislation, centralization of veterans' legislation in one agency is becoming an increasingly significant issue. For example, the expansion of federal support for health programs has raised the issue of whether health care programs for veterans should be centralized, or whether separate agencies should administer them. The expansion of public assistance and the rising levels of payments would apparently obviate the need for veterans' pensions. It is, however, more realistic to anticipate that veterans' organizations will continue to insist that separate programs be maintained for their clients, not only because these programs would provide more aid than that offered to other needy populations, but also because of the manner in which the programs are administered. As long as veterans' programs are administered with due regard for the dignity of the beneficiaries, their organizations will not lack support for separate programs.

Legislative Processing

The focal point of veterans' legislation since the end of World War II has been the House Committee on Veterans Affairs. Established in 1947, this committee has had jurisdiction over all veterans' legislation originating in the House. The veterans' organizations have found the committee sympathetic to their objectives and highly esteemed by the House establishment. Congressman Olin E. Teague of Texas chaired the committee between 1955 and 1973, and he was regarded by veterans' organizations as an ideal spokesman for their causes. Chairman Teague has been noted for his success in securing concensus among the 26 members of his committee. Legislation proposed by the House Veterans Committee has bipartisan support—neither party wants an antiveteran posture—and its bills are normally put on the House agenda under the suspension of rules procedure, precluding amendments from the floor. Members therefore have a choice of voting either for or against the legislation. This arrangement offers considerable advantage to some members, who have gone on record as favoring "more" than what was proposed by the bill. Under the circumstances, the closed rule must be a comforting security blanket. With no choice but to answer "yea" or "nay" Congressmen have a built-in alibi for delivering less than they had promised.

The Senate did not have a committee with exclusive jurisdiction over veterans' affairs until 1970, and legislation for veterans was assigned to the Senate committee responsible for the overall legislation in any given area. The Senate Committee on Finance handled pensions, compensation, and life insurance bills; the Committee on Labor and Public Welfare considered readjustment, rehabilitation, and medical programs; the Committee on Banking and Currency handled bills relating to housing and other guaranteed loans, and other committees got into the act as the occassion required.

Trying to centralize their programs under a single management, veterans' groups favored the creation of a Senate committee on veterans' affairs to parallel the jurisdiction of the House committee. The Senate committees involved were not enthusiastic about relinquishing jurisdiction over popular legislation, and the Senate Committee on Veterans Affairs was not established until the 1970 Legislative Reorganization Act. No doubt, the continued growth of outlays on veterans' programs added impetus to pull together the multibillion program under consolidated responsibility.

It appears, however, that the veterans' organizations may have gotten a different product than they bargained for. Initially, at least, the veterans' groups had ideological differences with the leadership of the Senate committee, chaired by Senator Vance Hartke of Indiana. But more important than ideological differences may have been the embarrassment caused when the Senate committee advocated much more liberal veterans' legislation than had been approved by the House. An early case in point was a bill to increase educational training allowances to veterans. The House approved a 14 percent increase in 1971, but the bill favored by Senator Hartke called for a 40 percent increase. Representatives of veterans' organizations who had acquiesced to much less than the Senate committee was willing to give them must have found it embarrassing when legislators outstripped organization demands. Off the record, representatives of veterans' organizations considered the Senate committee's generosity as bordering on "economic irresponsibility." As long as the Democrats retain control over the Senate, the committee is likely to remain a source of frustration and embarrassment to veterans' organizations.

Appropriations

In contrast to the perplexing liberal position taken by the Senate Committee on Veterans Affairs, the Office of Management and Budget has been irascibly tight fisted, becoming the traditional whipping boy of veterans' organizations. Regardless of the views held by the White House occupant at any given time, the executive branch has to play the unrewarding role of opposing liberalization of veteran benefits. It is the responsibility of the Office of Management and Budget to calculate projected costs of any programs considered by Congress, veterans' bills included. This is especially significant in the case of veterans' leglislation, where technicians must be on guard against "sleeper" clauses which may raise costs in future years. For example, a provision to liberalize pensions for Korean or Vietnam veterans might appear frivolous and of little cost if enacted by the 93rd Congress, because very few veterans would qualify initially under the liberalized benefits. The situation would change radically by the end of this century, but the chances of repealing legislation on behalf of veterans once it is enacted are very slim.

The Office of Management and Budget must recognize that the veterans' proposals it clears for congressional action are likely to become a floor on appropriations rather than a ceiling. The proposed budget for veterans therefore deviates from the usual practice, which is to allow for some fat in the executive budget to be trimmed by congressional economizers. The reverse is true for veterans' programs, where the administration can reasonably anticipate that its proposals will be sweetened by friendly congressional committees.

Appropriations hearings for most federally-supported programs frequently become adversary proceedings, with agency representatives defending their proposals, and congressional representatives searching for savings. The Veterans Administration representative appearing before appropriations subcommittees, in contrast, frequently finds himself in the position of having to oppose congressional largesse. Senator John O. Pastore of Rhode Island, in charge of the appropriations subcommittee that handled the VA budget for fiscal 1972, demonstrated the special treatment afforded VA representatives:

> *Senator Pastore:* You see, we take other agencies that come in over the coals, how many people they employ, what are they doing, why are they asking for so much more? These are questions that are never directed to the Veterans Administration, we take you on face value. . . .[14]

Sometimes the VA is taken at "face value" and then some. The Veterans Administration recommendations to Congress reflect White House budgetary decisions and the appropriations subcommittees take it upon themselves to ferret out the "real" recommendations of the Veterans Administration in order to give the agency all that it desires. The exchange of testimony over the reduction of the average daily patient load in VA hospitals from 83,000 to 79,000 exemplifies this reverse role.

> *Mr. Boland:* Let me ask you again, is this the result of the OMB or is it actually the recommendation of the VA?
>
> *Mr. Johnson:* It was a mutually arrived at determination of the patient census on which the medical care budget would be based.
>
> *Mr. Boland:* If you were to continue at your present level of operation throughout fiscal year 1972, how much additional funds would you require?
>
> *Mr. Johnson:* Close to $120 million.[15]

The budget which the House Appropriations Committee recommended added that sum to the OMB's recommendation and authorized an average daily patient load of 85,500.

The Senate subcommittee on VA appropriations, not to be outdone by its House counterpart, also pursued this line of questioning to ascertain if VA needs were being met. Senator Pastore pressed VA administrator Johnson whether he favored the additional appropriations recommended by the House. Aware that the administrator's responses would have to reflect official policy as approved by Office of Management and Budget, Senator Alan Cranston of California, chairman of the Senate Veterans Affairs Subcommittee on Health and Hospitals, was not satisfied, and he second-guessed Johnson's real wishes. Claiming that Johnson's request did not reflect the real needs of the Veterans Administration, Senator Cranston asserted that Johnson was "speaking under orders of the OMB after the VA had requested more authorization and had been turned down."[16] Not satisfied with the boost approved by the House, Cranston sought to triple it. Despite Johnson's disavowals, the final appropriation included a boost of $280 million over the administration request.

The Myriad Ombudsmen

The ombudsman idea is old hat to veterans. To provide service to veterans, the veterans' organizations have emphasized clearing the way of applicants in the bureaucratic maze, and a significant proportion of their budgets have been allocated to counseling veterans about their rights, and processing their applications for benefits.

The American Legion, Disabled American Veterans, Veterans of Foreign Wars, and other veteran organizations maintain service officers to act as "attorneys in fact" in helping veterans establish their claims. They are joined in this activity by the American Red Cross and other civic organizations. These services are performed free of charge and the Veterans Administration cooperates with the appropriate organizations by recognizing their service officers as accredited representatives. The VA also provides them with office facilities, and makes VA files and other pertinent government files available for their use provided the veteran has granted the service organization power of attorney. The organization represents the claimant until the final appeals board acts on the case.

States also operate departments to aid veterans in obtaining benefits. Forty-five states, the District of Columbia, Puerto Rico, the Virgin Islands, and Guam employed 770 accredited representatives in 1972. Including state-employed representatives, the Veterans Administration recognizes about 2,400 individuals who act as ombudsmen for veterans in cutting the red tape associated with the processing of applications.

The Veterans Administration itself has been sensitive to the difficulties faced by citizens attempting to get help from the government and has set up its own system of service officers whose major function is to help applicants. The VA employs in its regional offices, centers, and contact offices some 1,100 benefits counselors. The counselors serve primarily as technicians, providing the veteran information and helping him prepare applications for benefits in the most favorable light in order to maximize benefits.

The Veterans Administration also maintains a cadre of experienced service offices to assist congressional caseworkers. Constituents often appeal to their elected representatives for help in obtaining veterans' benefits and gaining access to veterans' hospitals. Caseworkers refer such requests to the VA liaison office for technical expertise in helping the constituent establish his claim. In effect, these service officers act as congressional intercessors and credit for a beneficial outcome is given to the congressman, contributing to the good will the VA enjoys on the Hill.

Despite these elaborate attempts to help veterans secure their rights, it became clear as the war continued that many Vietnam veterans were not reached by programs intended to help them. In the realization that it is not enough merely to have programs for a certain group of the population, but that it is also necessary to take special steps to bring these programs to their intended recipients, the VA embarked on an "outreach" program to aid veterans.

Attempts to inform GIs of their entitlements as veterans are made through military newspapers and radio announcements. VA representatives visit military bases, hospitals, and discharge points to help servicemen fill out advance applications. Once the GI is mustered out, the Department of Defense notifies the Veterans Administration, which contacts new veterans via letter informing them of potential benefits. The letters include return cards on which the veteran may indicate interest in some benefit or a desire to contact a VA service officer. In many areas veterans can make toll-free calls to service centers to inquire about benefits.

To help establish easy access, the VA opened special facilities to serve Vietnam veterans, known as United States Veterans Assistance Centers. Their major function is to assist veterans in obtaining not only VA services but also assistance from other agencies, including the Civil Service Commission, the Labor Department, and state or local public agencies and private groups. If the veteran does not contact the center, the special counselors assigned to the 72 centers, mostly in VA regional offices, go to him.

A Louis Harris survey of veterans' attitudes in 1971 suggested that the outreach activities are paying off. Veterans discharged within three years of the survey, and particularly those separated within the previous year, gave higher positive ratings to the VA for counseling veterans than veterans discharged prior to the initiation of the outreach activities. But many are still left out. More than one of every five indicated lack of information about available benefits and services. Apparently veterans who needed the help most were least aware of VA programs. Forty-three percent of veterans with a high school education or less stated that they have had almost no contact with the VA, compared to only 24 percent of those with some college and 31 percent of those with four years or more of college.[17] From the Harris survey, it is impossible to ascertain whether the contacts were limited by lack of effort or lack of interest, but certainly there seems to be less than complete success in the contact and outreach operation.

A Model Welfare System

Veterans' programs constitute a major part of the total welfare system, providing millions with income support, medical care, education and training, and means for acquiring housing and life insurance. These programs parallel provisions for the general public in social security, public assistance, health care, and housing programs, but in more generous dimensions.

The federal government has maintained a comparatively small bureaucracy to administer its programs, considering that 87 percent of the VA's 172,000 employees are engaged in the delivery of medical care. The agency administers vast programs with a relatively small number of people because it avoids the usual snooping and interminable paper shuffling associated with welfare programs. Indeed, the usual role of gum-shoeing for welfare cheaters is reversed. Congress deems all veterans deserving, and what investigative efforts the Veterans Administration staff conducts are more directed toward insuring veterans maximum benefits.

Large armies of volunteers augment Veterans Administration staff in delivery of benefits. Service organizations do a great deal of work that is usually performed by government officials in filing claims and generally aiding and comforting veterans. Veterans' programs experience genuine citizen participation and the American people have no qualms about delivering to veterans what is considered their just due. This system, which enjoys the good feeling of the people, the policymakers, and the program administrators, may serve as a model for the total welfare system. However, the American people do not accept the same criteria for administering benefits to the rest of the welfare population, and are likely to be unwilling to foot the bill for such a universal system.

CHAPTER 2

Income Support Programs

A man who is good enough to shed his blood
for his country is good enough to be given
a square deal afterward. More than that no
man is entitled to, and less than that no
man shall have.

Theodore Roosevelt
Speech at Springfield, Illinois
July 4, 1903

Transfer Payments for Veterans and Others

Income support for the aged, handicapped, and needy has been available to the population at large since the New Deal era; for veterans such support has been available since the birth of the nation. Cash payments to veterans are made either in the form of compensation or pension. Compensation provides income to veterans who suffered service-connected disability and to survivors of those who die as a result of military service. Disability compensation is an income supplement designed to reimburse the injured veteran for diminished earning power. It represents the nation's acceptance of its most obvious responsibility to those whose lives have been temporarily or permanently crippled by the government's decisions to wage war.

Pensions, on the other hand, provide income to veterans in need, even if this need does not stem from service to the country. The conditions for eligibility for this public support are wartime service, age or disability, and low income. Pensions are not delayed compensation or reimbursement for past service. They are income transfers to a chosen group, offered by a grateful nation to those in need. This distinction between the two kinds of assistance is important, because while compensation is an unassailable duty to the victims of war, pensions are need-based public support for veterans.

Like other welfare programs, income support to disabled and indigent veterans has accelerated in recent years. Total compensation and pensions paid to veterans from the inception of the program in 1790 to 1972 amounted to $106 billion. It is anticipated that income support outlays during the next decade will nearly equal the expenditures of the preceding two centuries. Veterans' income maintenance programs represent a major cost of past wars, and Congress has always been generous in paying that cost. In 1972 the VA outlays for compensation and pensions amounted to $6.2 billion, or more than half of the nation's expenditures in aid of veterans (table 2).

Veterans' income maintenance programs occupy a special position in the spectrum of federally supported income maintenance schemes. Veterans' compensation for death or injury parallels benefits required under state and federal compensation laws. Social security, which provides an income cushion to dependents of workers who have died or become totally and permanently disabled, also covers servicemen independently of veterans' benefits. Servicemen and their dependents may benefit simultaneously from two federal income support programs—one designed to protect the general population and the other specifically designed for members of the armed forces. Veterans' pensions parallel and frequently supplement the federal-state public assistance programs for the aged and disabled. Veterans' benefits, in effect, provide a separate "welfare" system to indigent veterans and their widows.

Compensation

The goal of compensation is to prevent destitution among veterans who have suffered a service-connected disability or among their surviving dependents. Two kinds of compensation are maintained by the government. Direct disability compensation to those with service-connected impairments, and continuing subsidies to dependent survivors of servicemen who die as a result of military service. Because direct compensation is partly an attempt to repay an incalculable social debt, the support is not subject to a means test and the disabled vet-

Table 2.   Income Support in 1972

Program	Cases (thousands)	Average Annual Payment	Cost (millions)
Total	4,792	—	$6,179
Compensation			
Veterans	2,122	$1,303	2,837
Survivors	372	1,879	700
Pensions			
Veterans	1,066	1,364	1,453
Survivors	1,232	859	1,058
Burial Awards and Other	—	—	131

Source: U.S. Congress, House Subcommittee of the Committee on Appropriations, HUD-Space-Science-Veterans Appropriations for 1973, 92nd Cong., 2nd sess., 1972, p. 949.

eran receives the compensation due him regardless of his income or assets. A disability rating schedule intended to measure the average earning impairment determines the level of payments made to the veterans.

A service-connected disability includes any impairment incurred by a serviceman which is the result of accident, injury, or disease that occurs during peace or wartime.[1] Under this definition, no qualitative distinction is made between the impairment of the serviceman who slips in his bathtub and the injuries suffered by the soldier who trips a mine while on patrol in Vietnam. A disability incurred while in service resulting from "willful misconduct" is considered nonservice-connected. Willful misconduct includes drunkenness, disobedience of orders, and the commission of crimes. A soldier disabled while AWOL, a deserter, or confined by civilian courts for a felony or by court martial involving dishonorable discharge is not considered to have incurred a service-connected disability. In effect, the government renounces its responsibility for later needs if the individual has not adhered to the rules of the military and the social system. A veteran forfeits all benefits if he receives a dishonorable discharge.

The law provides for a liberal definition of service-connected disability. Contraction of venereal disease while in service is not considered "willful misconduct" unless the soldier fails to report the disease and receive care. A disease which becomes evident while the individual is in service is presumed to be service-connected unless proof exists that the condition was present prior to induction. Induction physicals are designed to screen out individuals with such conditions. Certain disabilities which become manifest after discharge may also be considered service-connected. If the individual has served 90 days or more during wartime he is given the benefit of the doubt when a chronic disease surfaces, producing 10 percent or more disability within one year of separation from service. A veteran who served during a "period of war" who develops active psychosis within two years of discharge is considered to have a service-connected disability.

Determining Compensation Levels

A VA rating board made up of a physician, a lawyer, and an occupational specialist determines the extent of disability based on a "Schedule for Rating Disabilities," which lists specified disabling conditions from 10 to 100 percent. The scale primarily reflects impairment of ability to "perform manual labor," a concept dating from the era when most occupations called for physical skills. A "VA medical examination" is required prior to the award of compensation, but the

VA may accept any medical report from a government or private hospital in lieu of a VA examination.

Technically, admission to a VA hospital or a private facility at VA expense constitutes a basis for readjusting the compensation in light of new medical evidence and in some cases may result in termination. For instance, veterans with a 10 percent disability for malaria may be dropped from the compensation rolls if no symptoms recure within a year. However, the incidences of terminated compensation are rare. In 1971 only 6,046 out of more than 2 million cases were dropped from the rolls, and most of these were Vietnam era cases with temporary conditions. On the other hand, there were 55,000 new compensation recipients that same year. In 1972 a total of 2.2 million persons received compensation payments. World War II injuries still outnumbered compensation cases from all the other periods of war put together (chart 4). The average individual monthly compensation payment for each period of war was as follows:

War	Average Monthly Payments
All wars	$106
World War I	162
World War II	100
Korean Conflict	121
Cold War Era	96
Vietnam Era	117

The VA assigns ratings for every recognized disability. The calculation for determining the disability rating of a man who has incurred multiple distinct disabilities is based on the "whole man" approach which takes into account total impaired efficiency.[2] For example, a man with three distinct disabilities rated at 50 percent, 40 percent, and 20 percent would have his total disability computed on a compound basis. The first disability reduces his efficiency by 50 percent. The second disability lowers the remaining 50 percent efficiency by 40 percent and so on. In this case, the multiple factoring system results in a combined disability rating of 76 percent. The combined rating is rounded off to the nearest 10 percent for purposes of payment. Therefore, the man in the example would receive an 80 percent disability rating.

Monthly payments based on the 1972 schedule ranged from $28 for 10 percent disability to $495 for 100 percent disability, bringing maximum compensation to $5,940 annually (table 3). Compensation rates reflect the assumption that persons with less than 100 percent disability do not require proportionate support since they retain greater capability to take care of themselves. For example, payments

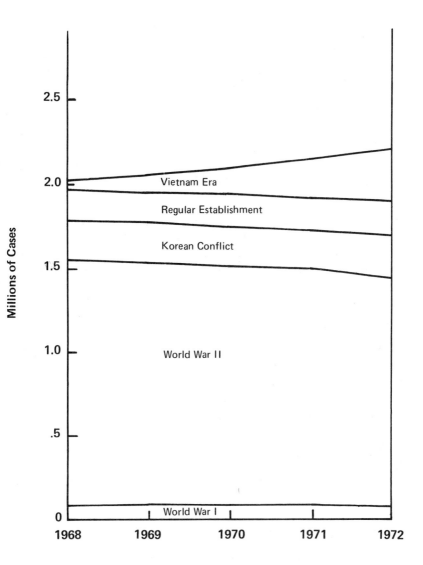

CHART 4

VIETNAM CASUALTIES ARE EXPANDING COMPENSATION ROLLS

Millions of Cases

2.5 —

2.0 — Vietnam Era

Regular Establishment

Korean Conflict

1.5 —

1.0 — World War II

.5 —

0 — World War I

1968   1969   1970   1971   1972

Source: Veterans Administration ·

34   OLD WARS REMAIN UNFINISHED

Table 3.   Partial Disability Is Compensated Proportionately Less than Total Disability

Percent of Disability	Monthly Payment	Monthly Payment as Ratio of 100 Percent Disability
10	$ 28	5.7
20	51	10.3
30	77	15.5
40	106	21.4
50	149	30.1
60	179	36.2
70	212	42.8
80	245	49.5
90	275	55.6
100	495	100.0

Source: U.S. Congress, House, *Compensation Rate Increases for Service-Connected Disabled Veterans: Public Law 92-382* (July 5, 1972).

for 50 percent disability amount to only 30 percent of the compensation paid for total disability.

The VA compensation makes allowances for shortening of life, social inconvenience, and pain or suffering associated with the disability. Veterans who have endured amputation, loss of senses, or loss of procreative power, are entitled to additional special monthly compensation. The monthly rate in 1972 was $47 for each disability, and greater sums for combinations of disability. The payment also recognizes extra costs of attendance required because of helplessness and inability to carry on with normal functions. In 1971, 154,000 veterans, or about 7 percent of compensation cases, received special statutory awards. Arrested tuberculosis cases rated at 0 percent disability accounted for nearly a fifth of all special statutory awards. The 0 percent disability rating is a holdover from a previous law which compensated veterans who once had service connected tuberculosis. Until 1968 veterans with completely arrested tuberculosis were entitled to $67 a month special compensation. The law was recinded but persons already on the rolls continue to receive the benefits. In 1972 the maximum monthly compensation and statutory award was $1,232. The relatively few disabled veterans receiving this income were, needless to say, severely damaged individuals.

Adequacy of Compensation

Most veterans were compensated for minor impairments. Forty percent were deemed to be 10 percent disabled, and their impairments to earning ability were often slight or hardly discernable. Removal of a knee cartilage, amputation of one finger or a big toe, impaired vision in one eye, dysentery, slight deafness in one ear, damaged facial muscles, or hemorroids usually qualified for the minimum disability rating. Fifty-six percent of veterans on compensation had less than 30 percent disability in 1971, and were not considered sufficiently handicapped to qualify for vocational rehabilitation. Amputation of an index and a little finger or all the toes on one foot, loss of muscle use in a foot or arm, visual impairment in both eyes up to 5/200, chronic laryngitis, or removal of the gall bladder or testis are examples of disabilities which could qualify for 30 percent disability rating. One of every five disabled veterans had impairments greater than 50 percent, qualifying them for additional compensation for their dependents. Complete deafness, partial blindness in both eyes, amputation of a hand or a leg above the knee, a collapsed lung, severely disfiguring scars, or paralysis of peripheral nerves were some of the disabilities which could be rated more than 50 percent disabling. Almost six percent of compensated veterans were 100 percent disabled, which meant that the individual had suffered loss of either two hands, or two feet, or a hand and a foot, or eyesight, or was rendered permanently helpless or bedridden (table 4).

Veterans who are 50 percent or more disabled are entitled to additional dependents' compensation based on the extent of their disability. Altogether 336,000 veterans claimed a total of 760,000 dependents in 1971 (including nineteen parents of W. W. I veterans), as follows: wives, 310,000; children, 432,000; parents, 18,000. The total added cost of dependents' compensation amounted to $136 million in 1971.

Table 4. Compensation Cases with Less than 30 Percent Disability Accounted for 56 Percent of the Cases but Only One-Sixth of All Payments in 1972

Percent Disability	Number of Cases (thousands)	Percent of Total Cases	Percent of Total Compensation Paid
Total	2,182	100.0	100.0
0	29	1.3	.8
10	861	39.5	9.3
20	338	15.5	6.7
30	310	14.2	9.4
40	176	8.1	7.5
50	112	5.1	7.6
60	111	5.1	12.5
70	69	3.2	9.7
80	35	1.6	5.3
90	12	.6	2.1
100	127	5.8	29.1

Source: Veterans Administration.
Note: Details may not add to totals because of rounding.

As of 1972, added monthly compensation for totally disabled veterans was $31 for a wife, $53 for a wife and child, and $67 for a wife and two children. This sliding scale added recognition of individual's varying responsibilities to the basic concept of lost earning power. A totally disabled veteran with a wife and two children received $6,744 compared to $5,940 for a single disabled veteran. Veterans disabled 50 percent or more who claim their parents as dependents may augment their compensation payment by as much as $25 a month for each parent depending on the extent of their disability. Income levels of parents claimed by veterans are not examined in determining dependence; the claim of the veteran is sufficient.

Replacement of lost earnings is a major function of compensation. A VA study published in 1971 tested the adequacy of compensation levels by comparing income of compensated individuals with the income of control groups. Of the disabled veteran population, 500,000 cases had 1,007 different single categories of disability. The control group was made up of 14,000 veterans with no service-connected injuries and was matched against test groups according to age, educational attainment, and region of residence. The annual income differential of veterans with distinct categories of disability was calculated by comparing income of the test groups with income of the control group. Although the findings show great variability in the income gap for specific categories, in about half of the disability categories the income of the control groups exceeded the income of disabled veterans by $1,000 or more. Altogether, 98.5 percent of the 1,007 test categories showed lower annual income than the control groups (chart 5).

The study examined the disability categories which most adversely affected earning ability, but did not indicate the distribution of veterans affected by these disabilities. Most severely affected were of veterans afflicted with mental disorders, pulmonary conditions, and epilepsies. For instance, the average annual income deficiencies for persons with psychotic disorders ranged from $1,093 to $7,100. A few examples selected from the 1,007 disability categories illustrate the range of economic loss due to disability (table 5). Persons who lost the use of a hand rated 60 percent disability. Veterans in this category suffered an annual income deficit of $2,000 after the $1,632 compensation was included in their total earnings. Persons who suffered amputation of a thumb or superficial scars incurred minor economic loss after compensation. According to the sample, persons with neuralgia of the sciatic nerve were better off economically than the control group.

The findings of the study are somewhat distorted because the tax-exempt status of compensation and the payment of additional family allowances and special compensation were not taken into account. The study also assumes that disabled veterans come equally

CHART 5

AVERAGE ANNUAL LOSS IN EARNINGS EXCEEDED $1,000 IN ABOUT ONE-HALF THE DISABILITY CATEGORIES

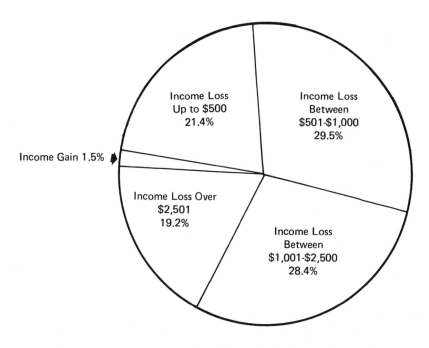

1,007 Disability Categories

Source: U.S. Congress, House Committee on Veterans Affairs, *Economic Validation of the Rating Schedule*, House Doc. no. 109, 92nd Cong., 1st sess., July 1, 1971, pp. 29–50.

from all income strata of the population and in the absence of war injuries would therefore have had the same earnings as their peers. Nonetheless, the study indicated a general pattern of lowered income levels for service disabled men. Since 1967, when the study data were collected, compensation levels have been raised. Increases in the cost of living, however, have eroded these gains and it is doubtful that most disabled veterans are any closer to income parity than before.

For the most disabled, the income deficiency is mitigated by eligibility for concurrent social security benefits. If a soldier was covered at the time of his disability by social security for at least six quarters he may receive at least $189.50 per month in social security benefits if he becomes totally disabled. VA compensation payments are

Table 5.   Most Disabled Veterans Had Less Income than Nondisabled Veterans in 1967 Even When Compensation Was Included

Category of Disability	Annual Compensation	Annual Income Deficit of Disabled Veterans after Compensation
Loss of use of hand (60 percent rating)	$1,632	$2,000
Amputation of thumb (40 percent rating)	984	33
Rheumatic heart disease (100 percent rating)	3,660	5,666
Neuralgia, sciatic nerve (30 percent rating)	720	−900[1]
Anxiety reaction (50 percent rating)	1,356	5,380
Scars, superficial (10 percent rating)	252	500

Source: U.S. Congress, House Committee on Veterans Affairs, *Economic Validation of the Rating Schedule,* House Doc. no. 109, 92nd Cong., 1st sess., July 1971, pp. 32, 40, 44, 47, 50.

[1] Indicates an income advantage; the disabled group had higher average income than the control group.

not counted as earned income and therefore do not offset social security. The additional stipend, while it clearly diminishes the income problems of the most crippled and bedridden, is not applicable to those who are only partly disabled. Since only 6 percent of VA compensation recipients are rated 100 percent disabled it seems likely that those with severe but not completely disabling impairments may be more economically squeezed than the most disabled.

VA Compensation in Perspective

To place VA compensation in the proper prospective, it might be useful to compare it provisions with other compensation plans. VA compensation for permanent partial and permanent total disability differs from most compensation programs in that payment schedules are based on extent of injury rather than percentages of salary scales. Federal employees disabled on the job receive benefits two-thirds to three-fourths of their salaries for the duration of the disability. Federally-regulated longshoremen's compensation pays two-thirds of the injured person's salary up to a maximum of $70 weekly. In cases of permanent partial disability, total maximum payment is $24,000.

State workmen's compensation laws vary widely, some paying flat rates, others a percent of salary. Nineteen states limit benefits to a specific period or amount payable to permanent total disability cases.[3] In cases of permanent partial disability, state laws often treat "schedule" injuries which are specific losses such as an arm amputation, differently from "nonschedule" injuries, which are more or less clearly defined, such as disability resulting from a trick knee. Thirty-seven states place time limits on compensation for "nonschedule" injuries ranging from 300 to 1,000 weeks. Twenty-one states limit total monies paid for any permanent partial disability.[4]

Compared with these programs run by the states, the provisions made for career servicemen by the Department of Defense are considerably more generous. Under the Uniform Services Career Compensation Act of 1949, servicemen who are retired by the military may elect to receive compensation from the Defense Department rather than from the VA. The VA standard schedule is used in rating disabilities, but the Department of Defense tends to be less liberal in determining ratings. However, since Defense compensation is based on pay rates, most officers and higher ranking enlisted men retiring with disabilities receive significantly higher payments than VA compensation.

In 1971 the Department of Defense paid $495 million to 128,000 permanently disabled retirees, an average of almost three times more per person than VA compensation.[5] Defense Department payments were significantly ahead of VA payments in nearly every category except the youngest and most disabled enlisted men. Under Defense disability compensation methods, a staff sargeant with 80 percent disability could receive a basic monthly payment of $378.10, while his VA payment would be $245.00 (although the VA payment might be supplemented for dependents or special injuries). A major with a 40 percent disability and 20 years of service could receive $659.50 per month in Department of Defense pay compared to $106 from the VA. The only levels at which basic VA compensation would exceed Defense Department disability pay would be for the lowest ranking enlisted men with the highest disabilities. For example, a private with less than two years of service and 100 percent disability would get $495 a month from the VA but only $250 if he qualified for disability retirement from the armed forces. (Both military and VA compensation payments are tax exempt.)

In addition, under the Defense Compensation Act a disabled serviceman with less than 30 percent disability is eligible for severance pay in lieu of disability payments. The lump sums are computed by multiplying years of service up to a maximum of 12 years by twice the monthly basic pay. For example, a colonel with 16 years of service retiring in 1972 with an ulcer could receive a lump sum of $37,648.00, the equivalent of forty years VA compensation. Evidently the military has persuaded Congress that disabilities incurred by higher ranking or longer term servicemen are deserving of much greater indemnities than those suffered by draftees and young enlisted men.

On the other hand, the law for veterans is more lenient than most state compensation plans in that there are no time or cumulative financial limits on compensation. Like all other workmen's compensation, VA compensation is not need based and is awarded equally to all, a recognition that loss of physical or mental integrity in war is a sacrifice which deserves equal compensation, regardless of previous income or future income prospects. The national responsibility fulfilled by VA compensation appears to be less one of replacing economic loss than of discharging a social debt to those disabled by war.

As a true compensation for loss, VA benefits appear to be less than satisfactory. First, they do not, even with social security additions, bring most disabled veterans up to parity with those who have not suffered injury. Second, the method of computation of disability fails to assess individual loss realistically. A pianist who loses three fingers is considerably more than 20 percent disabled. A computer programmer with the same disability may suffer no financial loss at all. An athlete who loses his chance to play sports ever again is not likely to feel that an extra $47 per month softens the blow very much. As thorny as this problem of varying loss may be, it would seem that some attempt to distinguish and define true economic and personal consequences might be made. VA compensation was designed at a time when tying benefit levels to pay scales might have worked a hardship on many men, especially those receiving lower than normal pay for their temporary service to the nation. The single-level-per-disability payments were aimed at universally recompensating disability at a rate as high as was feasible, considering budgeting constraints and the massive numbers of men involved. Clearly, since this beginning other programs involving smaller numbers of men in the military establishment have far outstripped VA compensation. Although present salary is one legitimate criterion for establishing potential economic loss, the vast disparities between individuals with identical disabilities do not appear just. Admittedly, career soldiers may deserve treatment different from those temporarily pressed into service. But a man in temporary service who is disabled for life has, in one sense, involuntarily become a career soldier, and deserves to be treated equally. VA compensation, which seems to be directed to more disabled, lower ranking servicemen, appears to need review and upgrading.

Survivor Benefits

Survivor benefits are cash stipends to widows, orphans, and dependent parents of deceased servicemen. Payments are in lieu of the dead serviceman's earnings and are designed to protect wives and children from economic deprivation. The provision for dependent parents compensates them for financial support they could have reasonably expected.

Some provision for compensation to dependent survivors of war servicemen has been on the law books since 1780. Initial assistance was limited to officers' widows, who were promised half their deceased husband's pay for a period of seven years. Universal compensation for widows of Revolutionary War casualties was delayed until 1836, when all widows were made eligible for pensions their husbands would have received. The laws were intended to offer some economic security to families of Revolutionary War veterans, although they were enacted more than half a century after the termination of hostilities. It is notable that the last Revolutionary War widow remained on compensation rolls until 1906.[6]

Currently, compensation to survivors is provided under two laws— death compensation, available to survivors of those who died before 1957, and dependency and indemnity compensation, paid to dependent survivors of servicemen who died from service-connected causes after 1957. Although generally more liberal than its predecessor, the dependency and indemnity law imposes income limitations on the eligibility of parents (though not on the widows or dependent children), and thus many parents have elected to continue to receive the earlier form of compensation.

Altogether, the VA administered 375,000 survivors' cases in 1972. About two-thirds received dependency and indemnity compensation and one-third remained on death compensation. A small percentage of cases involved split claims by widows and dependent parents, where widows elected dependency and indemnity compensation and parents independently elected death compensation. A total of 524,000 widows, children, and dependent parents of servicemen who died of service-connected causes received $700 million of compensation (table 6).

Benefits paid to widows are stopped upon remarriage, but may be resumed upon the termination of the remarriage. The children of servicemen retain eligibility for benefits until their 18th birthday, or 23rd if they continue their education. The law aims at preventing the

*Table 6.   Over 524,000 Surviving Dependents Received Compensation
            for Service-Connected Deaths in 1972*

(thousands)

Dependent	Total	World War I	World War II	Korea	Vietnam	Regular Establishment
Total	524	38¹	250	56	100	80
Widows	191	36	85	16	25	30
Children	124	1	23	12	54	34
Mothers	158	1	109	21	14	13
Fathers	51	¹	33	7	7	4
Percent of Total	100	7	48	11	19	15

Source: Veterans Administration.
Note: Details may not add to totals because of rounding.
¹ Includes 347 survivors of the Civil War and Spanish-American War servicemen and 36 fathers of World War I servicemen.

children of war casualties from becoming undue burdens even on stepfathers. Only in the case of dependent parents is eligibility conditioned on outside income. Parents may receive income support only if annual income falls below $2,600 for a single parent or $3,800 for both parents.

Until 1969, the basic dependency and indemnity support consisted of $120 a month, plus 12 percent of the basic pay scale adjusted for cost of living increases. This provision favored widows of servicemen in higher grades, who received increases in excess of living costs, while widows of servicemen in the lower grades were shortchanged.[7] The 1969 Dependency and Indemnity Compensation Act, though favoring widows of low-ranking servicemen, still related the level of support provided survivors to the earnings of the servicemen. Annual payments ranged in 1972 from $2,208 for a recruit's widow to $5,628 for the Chief of Staff's widow. The basic entitlement included an additional $20 a month for each child and $55 a month for a housebound widow in need of regular aid and attendance. Besides these changes, recent liberalizations of dependency and indemnity compensation income limitations have reduced the comparative advantage of death compensation in recent years even for dependent parents.

The Adequacy of Survivors' Compensation

Compensation is basically a work-related insurance policy designed to make military service more attractive by partially offsetting the increased occupational hazards. Coverage is more liberal and extensive than that found in other occupations, which require the the injury occur at work or because of conditions directly related to work. Death occurring "in line of duty" means any death occurring for a reason other than one's own misconduct. Military personnel are considered "on duty" at all times. Dependency and indemnity compensation follows the general pattern of survivors' benefits in federal and state compensation laws. Under the Federal Employment Compensation Act, the widow is entitled to 45 percent of her husband's salary during widowhood and up to 75 percent if two or more dependent children are involved. State laws vary in their provisions for widows and children. Widows' benefits range from one-third to two-thirds of the decedent's earnings and the percentage usually increases when dependent children are involved. In 36 states benefits are of limited duration and amount. In relative terms, then, dependency and indemnity compensation is more generous than state laws, but more restrictive than top federal employment compensation payments.

In absolute terms, the adequacy of survivors' compensation is marginal. Unlike direct compensation, survivors' benefits are allotted on a sliding scale depending on the pay grade of the deceased serviceman. Benefits paid to widows of the lowest ranking enlisted personnel barely exceed the 1973 federal poverty income threshold, set at $2,100 per year for a single urban female. For a woman with a child, whose husband had been ranked a corporal or less, benefit levels were below the poverty threshold of $2,725. For a widow with two children, the serviceman would have had to achieve the rank of sargeant major or above in order to bring dependency and indemnity compensation above the $3,450 poverty line.[8]

But most widows with minor children and those who were 62 years or older were also entitled to social security benefits. A widow with one dependent child was provided a minimum of $126.70 per month, while widows over 62 years of age who had no dependent children received a minimum monthly benefit of $84.48. The combination of social security and VA benefits has eliminated poverty for elderly widows and for service widows with young children.

Like other survivors' compensation laws, the VA dependency and indemnity legislation reveals ambivalence over the rationale behind the payments. Wives and children receive cash payments regardless of financial need. Parents, to whom society evidently feels less responsibility, receive only means-tested support. Apparently, the government's debt for the deaths of its soldiers remains flexible.

Given budgetary constraints, the government could adopt an alternative to the present compensation program by raising the benefits of those who need the help most. This approach would require a means test, which supporters of aid to dependents of war casualties find repugnant. Recognizing, however, that the government's debt of gratitude to the dead can never be fully repaid to the living, a system that would comfortably support all survivors in need may be preferable to the present modest help to larger numbers, including many who do not need the help.

Educational and Medical Care Benefits for Survivors

A special extension of survivors' compensation benefits was enacted in 1956, when the War Orphans' Educational Assistance Act made children of wartime casualties eligible to receive assistance for post-high school education and training. The legislation was later extended to dependents of totally and permanently disabled peacetime servicemen, to dependents of servicemen who died as a result of a service-connected disability, and to dependents of prisoners of war or servicemen missing in action. The survivors may be paid up to $220 per month for a maximum of 36 months of full time education.

A total of 168,000 children and 12,000 wives or widows had participated in the program by the end of fiscal 1971; the cumulative cost of subsistence allowances was $406 million. The VA anticipates a continuing increase in the number of wives or widows interested in using their eligibility. Also, the number of children participating will expand within the next few years as more survivors of World War II casualties finish high school.

Sixty-five thousand of the nearly one million potentially eligible survivors participated in the educational program in 1972. Only a fraction of the eligibles take advantage of educational benefits, either because most wives or widows are past their "educational" years, or because the educational aspirations of the children do not include college or post-high school vocational education.

Proposals to extend medical care to dependents of servicemen killed or totally disabled has followed the precedent of educational benefits. A 1972 bill would have provided medical care to this group of women and children, but was vetoed by President Nixon as part of his economy drive in the fall of 1972. Proponents of the legislation will no doubt revive the measure in the 93rd Congress.

Life Insurance

Provision for life insurance is a special application of compensation. The government got into the business of life insurance for servicemen during World War I. A shooting war is not an attractive risk for commercial life insurance and to provide an income cushion to veterans' dependents the government undertook the responsibility of selling insurance to World War I veterans. Having gone into the insurance business in 1917, the government continued to insure World War II and Korean servicemen. These policies did not end with the war, and the government found itself in the insurance business on a long-term basis.

In the 1950s, the Eisenhower administration tried to divest the government of economic activity in competition with private industry. The insurance business wanted to sell life insurance to veterans, but was not eager to take over war risks. The Solomonic solution was for private insurance to take over ordinary risks and for the government to assume responsibility for excess indemnities due to war casualties. In addition, the government retained insurance for disabled veterans who might also be considered poor risks by private companies.

Under the current Servicemen's Government Life Insurance (SGLI) program the serviceman is automatically insured for $15,000 at a premium charge of $2.55 a month, unless the individual makes a written statement declining coverage or electing reduced coverage. Practically all servicemen "volunteer" to avail themselves of this benefit. Upon discharge from the service, the veteran has the option of converting his life insurance policy to a private policy in one of the 600 approved insurance companies without having to undergo a physical examination. This allows the disabled man to purchase policies without having to pay higher premium rates. About one-third of veterans take advantage of the conversion option.[9]

In fiscal 1971 the government supplement to SGLI for extra hazard costs was $49.9 million above the income from premiums. With the decline of hostilities, it is anticipated that the government contributions will decline and hopefully will eventually be eliminated.

In addition to SGLI, the government operates five insurance programs that are holdovers from previous conflicts. At the end of 1971, these programs covered 5.4 million policies at the face value of $37 billion, or about 2 percent of all life insurance in force (table 7). Ex-

Table 7.   At the End of 1971 the VA Administered 5.4 Million Policies

Insurance Program	Policies in Force (thousands)	Amount of Insurance in force (millions)
Total	5,407	$36,925
United States Government Life Insurance (World War I)	181	776
National Service Life Insurance (World War II)	4,300	28,355
Veterans Special Life Insurance (Korean Conflict)	612	5,361
Service-Disabled Veterans Insurance	123	1,098
Veterans Reopened Insurance	191	1,335

Source: Veterans Administration, Government Life Insurance Programs for Veterans and Servicemen, Annual Report, 1971 (Washington: Government Printing Office, 1972), pp. 10–11.

cluding losses incurred through extra hazard deaths, VA expenses for administration of the government's life insurance programs amounted to $17.3 million in 1971. The extra hazard costs of disabled veterans' insurance are offset by earmarked appropriations. Also, profits accumulated from Korean Veterans Special Life Insurance have been siphoned off and applied to disabled veterans' insurance, thereby reducing the deficit. The total extra hazard costs amounted to $5.1 million in 1971. For the most part, profits from invested premium payments finance the veterans' life insurance programs.

Pensions

In addition to protecting most disabled servicemen and their survivors from poverty, the government offers extensive income support to indigent veterans and their needy survivors. The welfare system available to veterans is much more generous than the public assistance system that serves other poor people, and the pensions paid to veterans may be added to their other income support programs. Indeed, a veteran's income may exceed the poverty threshold, but he may still qualify for a pension. In 1972, the Veterans Administration distributed $2.5 billion to 2.3 million beneficiaries. The present magnitude of the programs is the result of constant growth since World War II.

Early precedents, the evolution of old laws, and the expansion of general social welfare programs have resulted in several pension programs for veterans. Universal service pensions are provided for "old war" veterans, meaning Spanish-American War and Indian War Veterans, while means-tested, nonservice-connected disability pensions are available to veterans of World War I and later conflicts. The same rules apply to the survivors of veterans.

Under the present system, pensions are a gratuity, not a legal right. Only the VA appeal system has authority to grant or deny a pension. Eligibility depends upon disability and need, and applies to veterans and survivors alike.

The pension programs for veterans reflect changing social conditions. Although veterans' pension programs pioneered social welfare provisions for a segment of the population, maturation of the social welfare system has diluted the basis for this separate system. The passage of the Social Security Act in 1935 and its subsequent expansion, and the development of federal and state public assistance programs potentially provide income to the same general target population. Retirement provisions for career military personnel and for growing numbers of wage and salary workers have spread earned income over retirement years. Women's new place in the labor market has meant that surviving wives and mothers of veterans are not automatically dependent on the state. Moreover, veterans are no longer a small group. Nearly half of the men in the United States over 18 are veterans, compared with one of every eight prior to the end of World War II. Never before had such a large proportion of the population been potentially eligible for benefits.

Eligibility criteria for VA pension programs are the most liberal among means-tested programs for the poor. "The dollar amounts of the needs test were set," according to a top VA official, "at a level high enough to insure against anyone confusing the pension program with charity, or of associating the receipt of pension with indigency."[10] An examination of the various programs lends support to Gilbert Y. Steiner's description of veterans' relief as a "separate and unequal" welfare system.[11]

Veterans' Pensions

The government has rarely taken away a special privilege or benefit once a group is singled out to receive favors. Often benefits are extended to more, rather than fewer, recipients. Spanish-American War soldiers were pensioned in 1920, 21 years after the close of the war. Eligibility criteria consisted of 90 days of service, an honorable discharge, and either disability incapacitating the veteran for manual labor or attainment of 62 years of age. In 1958, legislation eliminated all criteria except the duration of service standard, and that was lowered to 70 days. The establishment of a universal service pension 58 years after the war followed the pattern of providing income support for surviving veterans four and five decades after the conclusion of the war. Of the 4,000 Spanish-American War veterans still living in 1971, 3,318 received pensions.

The era of general service pensions ended with Spanish-American War veterans. Try as they might, veterans of World War I have been unable to convince Congress to delete the means test placed on pensioners of "new wars." To qualify for pensions, veterans of World War I, World War II, Korea, and Vietnam must meet a combination of service, disability, age, and need tests. Persons with 90 days of wartime service who are disabled and cannot work or are over 65 years and whose income is below the "need" standard qualify for a pension. Under the law, persons are considered totally and permanently disabled for purposes of employment at 65 years and no physical examinations is required. Those younger than 65 must show substantial disability and evidence of unemployability in order to qualify for pensions. Demonstration of unemployability is based on an examination of employment history. If the individual has been unable to hold down other than marginal employment, defined as working less than half the usual hours or earning less than half the going wage, he is judged eligible.

The majority of pensioners in 1972 were World War I veterans (chart 6). Their average age in 1972 was 78 years and their numbers were rapidly diminishing. World War II veterans make up the next largest group of pensioners, and their numbers are on the rise as more reach the age where physical infirmities increase and income declines.

Disability assistance to veterans under 65 parallels similar social security benefits and aid to the totally and permanently disabled under the public assistance system. The average pensioner in 1971 was 68 years old and two-thirds of the recipients were 65 and older (table 8). The pattern of disability rating varies by age. Nearly all the pensioners under 55 years were at least 50 percent disabled, while a third of the pensioners 65 and over were in that category. Few veterans,

CHART 6

THE MAJORITY OF PENSION RECIPIENTS IN JUNE 1972 WERE WORLD WAR I VETERANS

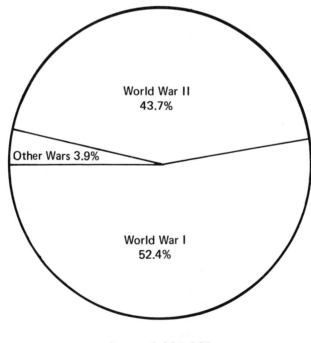

World War II
43.7%

Other Wars 3.9%

World War I
52.4%

Total: 1,086,000

Source: Veterans Administration.

Table 8.   *The Majority of Pensioners in September 1971 Were over 65 Years Old*
          and Most Were Disabled 50 Percent or More

Age	Number of Veterans (thousands)	Percent of Total	Percent Disabled 50 Percent or More
Total	1,080	100.0	76
Under 34	3	.3	99
35 to 44	41	3.8	99
45 to 54	150	13.9	96
55 to 64	158	14.6	93
65 and Over	728	67.4	68

Source: Veterans Administration, "Disability Pension: Age and Combined Degree of Impairment," unpublished paper RCS 21–24, September 1971.

unless they are totally incapacitated, qualify for pensions prior to age 65. The disability pattern reflected regulations requiring high disability levels in addition to low income for those under 65 years. Able-bodied adult men are not eligible for income support.

"Need" is set by income limits of $2,600 for a single veteran and $3,800 for a veteran with a dependent under the "new law" enacted in 1960, and $1,900 and $3,200 for veterans who elected to remain pensioned under the "old law" in effect prior to 1960. The program is administered with due regard to the dignity of the recipients and, unlike the public assistance system, the means test is not mean. All a veteran has to do to maintain eligibility for a pension is to submit an annual income statement indicating earned income of the past year and anticipated income in the upcoming year. If the veteran is 72 years old and has been on pension rolls for two consecutive years, he is exempted from filing income reports.

Certain general income exceptions are permitted in calculating income and these are significantly more liberal than the prevailing practices under public assistance. Ten percent of social security or any other retirement income is not counted. Income support from friends, relatives, or organizations is excluded, as are public assistance payments and the earnings of minor family members.

Until July 1, 1960, qualifying veterans received uniform pensions. The 1960 law provided for a "sliding scale" based on the recipient's other income. The new system of differential rates provides greatest assistance to the most needy.

To insure that no one received less income under the new law, pensioners already on the rolls could choose the system they preferred. The old law provided in 1972 for an annual pension of $945 to a veteran who was single and had income below $1,900. The income limit was $3,200 if he had a dependent. Earnings of the spouse were excluded and the value of the veteran's estate was not considered.

In contrast, the 1960 law counts all the spouse's annual income above $1,200 and the veteran's assets from which he can draw support are considered in establishing eligibility. According to VA administrator Donald E. Johnson, "Persons receiving protected pension under the prior law have enjoyed a favored status over current law pensioners because of more effective tests of need under the new program."[12]

The benefit schedule in 1972 under the 1960 law provided a single veteran a maximum annual payment of $1,560 and a veteran with a dependent up to $1,680. The maximum monthly benefit, equaling $130 for a single veteran and $140 if he had one dependent, was reduced in relation to outside income according to a formula (table 9). The average annual "new" pension in 1972 was $1,114 for a single veteran and $1,436 for a veteran with a dependent. A single veteran, for example, with an annual income of less than $300 was entitled to the maximum pension of $1,560 a year. If his income rose to $2,000, his pension would have been reduced by $816 (36 percent of $700 + 48 percent of $500 + 60 percent of $300 + 72 percent of the final $200), leaving him an annual income of $2,744. The 1960 law was designed to provide greater income to the very poor, but does not terminate benefits until outside income exceeds $2,600 for the single pensioner and $3,800 if he has a dependent, appreciably above the poverty thresholds (chart 7). Despite more stringent examination of estate values and consideration of spouses' income, the new pension system was favored by most pensioners.

The VA does not scrutinize income reports and respondents are

Table 9. In 1972 Pensions to Veterans under the 1960 Law Were Reduced in Relation to Outside Income According to a Formula

Annual Outside Income	Marginal Tax Rate	Pension
Single Veteran		
Up to $300	0	$1,560
$301 to $1,000	36	$1,559–$1,308
$1,001 to $1,500	48	$1,307–$1,068
$1,501 to $1,800	60	$1,067–$888
$1,801 to $2,200	72	$887–$600
$2,201 to $2,600	84	$599–$264
Above $2,600	100	0
Veteran with One Dependent		
Up to $500	0	$1,680
$501 to $900	24	$1,679–$1,584
$901 to $3,200	36	$1,583–$756
$3,201 to $3,800	60	$755–$396
Above $3,800	100	0

CHART 7

PENSIONS ARE REDUCED AS OUTSIDE INCOME INCREASES

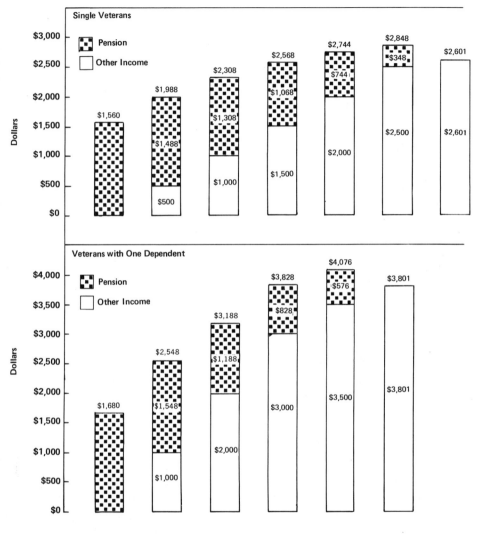

Source: Veterans Administration.

assumed to be truthful. However, General Accounting Office reports has substantiated underreporting of income in order to qualify for pension rolls. The GAO has criticized the VA's reporting requirements and has charged the VA with laxity in reviewing pension applications. It has recommended that the VA develop more stringent procedures

*Table 10.   Veterans with Less than $1,000 Outside Annual Income Received
about Two-Fifths of Direct Pension Dollars in 1972*

Non-VA Income	Number of Cases (thousands)	Direct Pension Payments[1]	
		Amount (millions)	Percent
Total	900	$1,140	100.0
Single Veterans	316	390	
Up to $300	86	134	11.7
$301 to $1,000	69	96	8.4
$1,001 to $1,500	77	91	8.0
$1,501 to $1,800	37	36	3.2
$1,801 to $2,200	38	29	2.5
$2,201 to $2,600	10	5	.4
Veterans with Dependents	584	749	
Up to $500	73	122	10.7
$501 to $900	43	69	6.1
$901 to $3,200	438	539	47.3
$3,201 to $3,800	30	19	1.6

Source: Veterans Administration, Department of Veterans Benefits, unpublished data, caseload of April 30, 1972.
Note: Details may not add to totals because of rounding.
[1] Direct pension payments exclude costs of aid and attendance.

for reviewing applications, verifying actual income, and providing pensioners with more detailed instructions for preparing their income questionnaires.[13]

Of the $1,140 million distributed in 1972 to veterans pensioned under the new law, $391 million went to single veterans and $749 million to veterans with dependents. About two-fifths of the funds went to veterans who reported $1,000 or less outside income (table 10).

Pensions for Dependents

Traditionally, the government has maintained an income maintenance program for veterans' widows and dependent children in addition to pensions paid directly to needy veterans; however, the level of support to survivors is less than that to veterans. As with other veterans' benefits, provisions for widows vary according to war, reflecting changing governmental policies, the development of other welfare provisions for women, and the changing role of women in the work force.

Women are eligible by virtue of former marriage status and present economic need. Conditions of old age or dependent children are not mandatory, though they frequently apply. General eligibility for any survivors' pension requires that the widow was married to the veteran before a specified date, a provision which prevents mercenary marriages to qualify for benefits. Children are eligible if they are under 18 years, or under 23 if attending school, or indefinitely if they become permanently disabled while receiving benefits.

The price tag of survivors' benefits in 1972 was $1,058 million, shared by 1.9 million widows and children. The average monthly payment was $70.[14] The majority of beneficiaries were survivors of World War II veterans, most of whom were children, while World War I beneficiaries were largely aging widows (chart 8). Like veterans' pen-

CHART 8

RECIPIENTS OF SURVIVORS PENSIONS NUMBERED 1,866,000 IN 1972

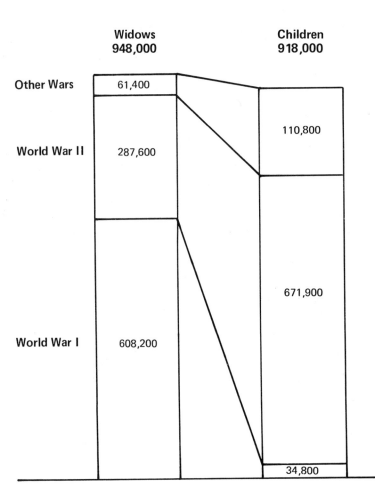

Source: Veterans Administration.

sions, survivors' pensions were paid under two laws. Under the "old law," a widow in 1972 received an annual pension of $605, or $756 if she had a dependent. Dependents of Spanish-American War veterans received somewhat higher payment.

The 1960 "new law" provided payments on a sliding scale and the average annual amount paid to a widow was $813, or $1,088 to a widow with one dependent. The maximum annual payment in 1972 of $1,044 for a single widow and $1,248 for a widow with one dependent was reduced in relation to other income, again according to a formula (table 11). An additional annual stipend of $206 was added for each dependent. In 1972, $697 million was expended for direct survivors' pensions, not including aid and attendance costs and costs for additional dependents; $541 million went to single widows, and $166 million to widows with minor dependents. About one-fourth of the funds went to widows with outside income below $600 (table 12).

An attempt was made after World War II to limit the numbers eligible for pensions, qualifying only widows of World War II and Korean Conflict veterans who had been entitled to compensation or disability retirement. A means test was also applied. Provisions established in the 1944 GI Bill would have limited survivors' pensions to about 7 percent of the potential veteran population. The provision in effect singled out a special class in recognition of the husbands' diminished earning power due to war injury. This policy was reversed in 1959, qualifying all indigent veterans' survivors for pensions. The result was the addition by 1971 of over 266,000 World War II, Korean, and Vietnam era survivor pensions cases, making up nearly a third of pensioned widows and over 90 percent of widows' dependents.

Table 11.   In 1972 Pensions to Widows under the 1960 Law Were Reduced According to a Formula

Outside Income	Marginal Tax Rate	Pension
Widow Alone		
Up to $300	0%	$1,044
$301 to $600	12	$1,043–$1,008
$601 to $1,900	36	$1,007–$540
$1,901 to $2,600	48	$539–$204
$2,601+	100	0
Widow with One Child		
Up to $600	0	$1,248
$601 to $1,400	12	$1,247–$1,152
$1,401 to $2,700	24	$1,151–$816
$2,701 to $3,800	36	$815–$420
$3,801+	100	0

*Table 12.   About One-Fourth of Direct Survivor Pension Dollars Went to
Widows with Less than $600 Outside Income*

| | Number of Cases (thousands) | Direct Pension Payments[1] | |
Non-VA Income		Amount (millions)	Percent
Total	805	$697	100.0
Single Widows	652	531	
Up to $300	118	124	17.8
$301 to $600	21	21	3.1
$601 to $1,900	466	365	52.4
$1,901 to $2,600	47	20	2.9
Widows with Dependent	153	166	
Up to $600	25	31	4.5
$600 to $1,400	53	64	9.2
$1,401 to $2,700	56	59	8.5
$2,701 to $3,800	18	12	1.7

Source: Veterans Administration, Department of Veterans Benefits, unpublished data, caseload of April 30, 1972.
Note: Details may not add to totals because of rounding.
[1] Direct pension payments exclude costs of aid and attendance.

It was anticipated that the development of the welfare system as envisioned by the Social Security Act of 1935 would obviate the need for a means-tested nonservice-connected pension program. A thorough and sympathetic study of the veterans' welfare system conducted by a presidential commission headed by General Omar N. Bradley concluded in 1956:

The non-service-connected benefits are the lowest priority among veteran's programs. Their justification is weak and their basic philosophy is backward looking rather than constructive. Our society has developed more equitable means of meeting most of the same needs and big strides are being made in closing remaining gaps. The non-service-connected benefits should be limited to a minimum level and retained only as a reserve line of honorable protection for veterans whose means are shown to be inadequate and who fail to qualify for basic protection under the general Old-Age and Survivors Insurance system.[15]

Whatever the merits of this recommendation, the Bradley Commission did not reckon with the difficulties inherent in terminating a social program. The commission underestimated the ability of the pension clientele and its supporters to raise pension levels and to insist that VA assistance remain more attractive than the income support available to the rest of the population.

Social Security

Most pensioners, both veterans and survivors, have income from
other sources, including social security, private pensions, and wages.
Data based on a 1 percent sample of the benefit population found that,
in 1970, 94 percent of those pensioned under the "old law" and 86
percent pensioned under the "new law" reported that they had other
sources of income (table 13). The 1970 sample also revealed that about
6 percent of the recipients had income before pension which exceeded
eligibility cutoff points effective in 1970.

The most important source of income available to potential pension recipients is social security. While the latter is essentially an insurance progam, in that employers and employees finance the program,
it also achieves some redistribution. Although social security benefit
schedules are a function of past earnings, they favor lower earners.

Monthly benefits under the 1972 law ranged from a minimum of
$84.50 per month to a maximum of $259.00, and averaged $161. Pay-
ments are subject to curtailment when earned income passes $2,100 at
a marginal tax rate of 50 percent, and at the rate of 100 percent on
earnings over $3,300. Persons over 72 years old who did not earn
coverage are entitled to monthly payments of $58.70, and reductions
of benefits on earnings are dropped after the recipient reaches 72 years
of age. Average social security benefits are adequate to raise most of
the aged above the poverty threshold, but many who depend solely
upon social security and receive below-average benefits remain in
poverty.

Benefits paid to totally disabled persons are the same as for retirement insurance. Medical qualifications are more stringent than disability levels for VA pensions. Disability must be total and continuous
for at least a year. Recipients can earn additional income up to $175 a

Table 13.   Income of VA Pensioners from Other Sources

Income Sources	Percentage of Total Recipients "New Law"	Percentage of Total Recipients "Old Law"
Old Age and Survivors Insurance[1]	74.7	82.9
Only OASI	48.1	34.7
OASI and Wages	4.9	6.4
OASI and non-VA Pension	10.8	19.0
OASI and Other	16.8	32.4
Other Income	11.3	11.5
No Outside Income	14.0	5.6

Source: Veterans Administration, unpublished data from 1 percent sample of the
1970 annual income questionnaire.
[1] Details do not add up to 100 percent because of multiple income sources.

month. When earnings exceed that amount, disability benefits are reduced by one dollar for every two earned.

Three of every four veteran pensioners receive social security benefits, but only 90 percent of that amount is counted as earned income for determining eligibility and level of pensions. However, the Social Security Administration does not count VA pensions as earned income and pensions do not affect the level of social security payments.

Because social security benefits are based on contributions and are not a gratuity, veterans' groups are currently arguing for deletion of such benefits from earned income on which pension rates are fixed. The VA estimated in 1969 that if such legislation were enacted, the cost would exceed a billion dollars per year. The 15 percent hike in social security benefits in 1969 reduced pension payments in 69 percent of the cases.[16] Consequently, Congress increased income limitations by $300, effective January 1, 1972, and the payment formula was redesigned so that aggregate income of pension recipients would not decrease as the result of increased income from any source as long as total income did not exceed maximum annual limitations. The 1972 boost in social security has prompted proposals to further liberalize the income limitations to prevent the disqualification of 20,000 pensioners whose income was raised above the limit by the new social security benefits.

The redesigned pension system allows it to act in tandem with social security, giving the greatest income support to veterans with the least outside income. If the veteran qualifies for both income support systems, with minimum social security payments, his annual income would be $2,353.44, as follows:

Minimum annual social security benefit for single retired worker	$1,014.00
Maximum VA pension	1,560.00
90 percent of social security benefits are counted as "other income" which in this case equals $912.60, and VA pension is reduced by 36 percent of income between $300 and $1,000 (36 percent of $612.60)	—220.54

Since social security extends to over 90 percent of the work force, the combination of systems has virtually eliminated poverty among old and disabled veterans.

Social Security benefits ranged in 1972 from $126.70 to $375.80 a month for a widow with one minor dependent. VA widows' pensions are not cut off when their children reach maturity and then resumed after reaching old age, as is the case with social security benefits.

For a widow with one dependent who qualifies for both benefits, the minimum income support is $2,676.24, as follows:

Minimum social security benefits for a widow and one minor dependent	$1,520.40
Maximum VA benefit for widow and one minor dependent	1,248.00
90 percent of social security benefits is counted as "other income," which equals $1,368.36 in this case, and the VA survivors' pension is reduced by 12 percent of income between $600 and $1,400 (12 percent of $768.36)	—92.16

For an aged widow with no dependents, the combination of the two income maintenance systems would provide a minimum of $1,880.00:

Minimum social security benefit to a widow over 62 years of age	$1,014.00
Maximum VA payment to a widow alone	1,044.00
90 percent of social security benefits are counted as "other income," which in this case equals $912.00, and the VA pension is reduced by 12 percent of income between $300 and $600 and 36 percent of income between $600 and $1,900 (12 percent of $300 plus 36 percent of $312)	—66.00 —112.000

Both systems provide lower income support to aged widows than is available to the retired worker or veteran. The combination of the two systems generally places recipients above the poverty threshold and thus disqualifies them for other public assistance payments.

The Bradley Commission envisoned that social security benefits would gradually eliminate the income support role of veterans' pensions. Congress, however, has not seen fit to let the general program supersede special veterans' benefits and has enacted legislation after each boost in social security payments to insure that veterans are not denied their special benefits.

Persistence of Poverty

A minority of veterans and their survivors are not covered by social security, and pensions help most, but not all, of them to escape poverty. While the veterans' pension system may be regarded as a generous means-tested program, the level of payments to those completely destitute is not adequate to pull all eligible veterans above poverty. Single veterans whose income was below $550 and veterans with dependents whose income was below $950 were not raised above the poverty threshold by their VA pension. Out of the 197,000 veterans drawing pensions in 1971 under the "old law," the income of 28 percent remained below the poverty threshold. The "new law" made more liberal provision for the veteran without income, but still 32 percent of all single veterans and one of every four veterans with dependents drawing pension remained in poverty (table 14). At the other end of the pension income spectrum, one of every eight veterans receiving pensions was above the poverty threshold prior to receipt of VA payment. More significant, however, is the fact that the pensions pulled 60 percent of all recipients from the ranks of the poor.

The VA data tend to overestimate the extent of poverty that still prevails among veterans, since some of the income received by veterans is disregarded for purposes of calculating pension payments. Most significant are the disregard of 10 percent social security benefits, the first $1,200 of the spouse's income, and all public assistance payments. Given these disregards, it would appear that the veteran welfare system virtually eliminates poverty among aged and disabled veterans.

Since payments to survivors are lower than pensions for veterans and a smaller proportion of survivors have outside income, a significant proportion of the beneficiaries remain poor even after receipt of pensions. Only half of the 105,000 widows qualifying for survivors'

Table 14. The Majority of Recipients under the 1960 Law Rose above Poverty in 1971 by Virtue of Their Pensions[1]

Annual Counted Income	Annual Pension	Number of Recipients (thousands)	Poverty Status[2] of Recipients
Veterans Alone		305	
Below $550	$1,380 to $1,452	97	32% remained in poverty
Between $550 and $1,949	684 to 1,344	192	63% raised above poverty
Between $1,950 and $2,300	384 to 612	16	5% were above poverty prior to pension
Veterans with Dependents		567	
Below $950	1,380 to 1,584	144	25% remained in poverty
Between $950 and $2,450	972 to 1,428	334	59% raised above poverty
Between $2,451 and $3,500	408 to 936	89	16% were above poverty prior to pension

Source: Veterans Administration. Unpublished, mimeographed data from 1971 annual income questionnaire.

[1] The 1971 figures reflect the payment schedule in effect prior to the liberalized payment formula effective January 1, 1972.

[2] The poverty status of recipients was computed by comparing income before and after pension to poverty thresholds determined by the Bureau of the Census.

benefits in 1971 under the "old law" reported income after pension exceeding the poverty threshold. The "new law," under which 88 percent of survivors received pensions, was even less effective. In 1971, the "new" sliding payments were sufficient to raise a single widow with an outside income of $1,150 or a widow with a dependent child who had an outside income of $1,650 above the poverty level. But nearly two of every three lone widows and three of every four widows with dependents reported income below these levels to the VA (table 15).

Public Assistance

Although social security is a more important source of income to veterans and their dependents, the public welfare system might be a more appropriate parallel to veterans' pensions than the social security program. Eligibility for both public assistance and pensions is based on need. Since public assistance is administered by the states, conditions for eligibility and levels of support vary. The criteria for eligibility are more demeaning, however, and in some states levels of support are more niggardly than VA benefits. In July 1971, maximum for old age assistance payments for an aged woman ranged from $75 a month in Mississippi to $250 in Alaska. The median maximum payment was $130. Maximum aid to the disabled ranged from $66 to $250 a month, with a median maximum payment of $122 per month. Generally, veterans' survivor pensions were inferior to payments provided under public assistance, while veterans' pensions payments were generally higher. By 1974, all recipients of old age, blind, or disabled public

Table 15. *"New Law" Survivors' Pensions Failed To Raise the Majority of Recipients above the Poverty Threshold in 1971*

Annual Counted Income	Annual Pension	Recipients (thousands)	Poverty Status of Recipients
Widows Alone			
Below $1,150	$732 to $ 972	381	63% remained in poverty
$1,151 to $1,950	396 to 696	212	35% raised above poverty
$1,951 to $2,300	204 to 348	11	2% were above poverty prior to pension
Widows with One Dependent			
Below $1,650	984 to $1,188	107	73% remained in poverty
$1,651 to $2,550	768 to 960	24	17% raised above poverty
$2,551 to $3,500	492 to 744	15	10% were above poverty prior to pension

Source: Veterans Administration, unpublished data from 1971 annual income questionnaire.

assistance will receive a minimum of $130 a month for a single person and $195 a month for a couple, which will minimize the economic advantage of veterans' pensions.

Public assistance eligibility is restricted by property, assets, and income limits. States may allow recipients to own their home and property limited to $1,200 in value. In 31 states, the granting of public assistance constitutes a lien against the property of the recipient, effectively denying property rights to the poor. Additionally, the tax on earnings or other outside income above $30 per month and work-connected expenses is 67 percent and may act as a work disincentive.

Veterans' pensions include no such demeaning stipulations. The determination of net worth limitation is subjective. There is no pre-scribed dollars and cents limit. An individual's assets are judged by type and amount, and whether they can be easily converted into cash without causing undue hardship to the owner. The pensioner is not required to sell his home and, generally, ownership of nonincome-producing assets does not bar pension payments. The individual's age, number of dependents, his health, and the health of his dependents are all considered in assessing net worth and future economic needs of the individual and whether his estate should "reasonably" contribute to his support. If liquidation of the estate would prove excessively burdensome, it is the VA's policy not to require it.

As we have seen, widows' pensions are less generous than veterans' stipends. The top monthly rate for a single widow is $87, as compared to $130 for a single veteran. Moreover, the asset and income limitations are more stringent for widows. The program provides primarily old age assistance; two-thirds of the pensioned widows are over 65. Old Age Assistance (OAA), Aid to the Totally and Permanently Disabled, and Aid to Families with Dependent Children (AFDC) extend assistance to similar populations as are aided by widows' pensions. Even public assistance is more generous than widows' pensions, which are lower than maximum public assistance benefits provided in all but three states. The average monthly VA widows' pension in 1971 was $65, compared with the average OAA payment of $76.

About 17 percent of pensioned widows have dependent children. In 1971 the maximum VA monthly payment to a widow with one child was $104. AFDC payments, which are the least generous of the public assistance programs, averaged a maximum of $153 monthly for a mother and child. The range of payments under AFDC varies radically from a maximum payment in 1972 of $30 per month in Mississippi to $255 a month in Michigan. Nonetheless, the treatment accorded pen-sioners differs radically from that accorded public assistance recipients. Pensions are regarded as gratuities in recognition of past services, to protect this deserving portion of society from facing the "ugly specter" of public charity. Recipients of public assistance, on the other hand, are somehow guilty of inadequacy and are blamed for their misfortune.

Despite the presumed liberality of veterans' pensions, those with no other income but VA payments qualified, on the basis of income, for old age assistance in 31 states. Single pensioned widows with no other income qualified for old age assistance in all states but South Carolina. About 12 percent of all persons receiving VA pensions, some 291,000 persons, also received public assistance payments. There is evidence that many more veteran pensioners qualify for public assistance but do not take advantage of the benefits, reflecting the prevailing attitude toward "being on welfare."

Past Experience and Projections

Between 1960 and 1972, the number of compensation and pension recipients has increased from 3.9 million to 4.9 million. Pensions cases accounted for most of the rise, since the number of veterans and widows receiving compensation has remained fairly stable. The 5 percent increase in the compensation caseload which has occurred since 1970 reflects Vietnam veterans coming on the rolls faster than veterans of previous wars are dying off. The pension caseload for World War I veterans and survivors peaked in the middle sixties. The 1959 law qualified indigent widows and children of World War II, Korean, and, later, Vietnam veterans to receive pensions. Prior to the passage of this law, only dependents of service-disabled veterans and all indigent dependents of World War I and earlier wars were eligible to qualify for pension. This effected a dramatic increase in survivor pension cases.

While the caseload of VA income maintenance programs increased by 25 percent between 1960 and 1972, the costs rose 83 percent, largely as a result of higher benefits (chart 9). The biggest increases occurred in nonservice-connected benefits. Flat rate pension payments were changed to graduated income support, greatly increasing the potential level of payments. While the 1959 law tightened income restrictions to qualify for veterans' pensions, it greatly expanded the population eligible for widows' pensions. The cost of pensions increased 59 percent between 1960 and 1972 and the cost of survivors' pensions soared 200 percent.

The Vietnam war added compensation cases and potential claimants for pensions. Barring future changes in eligibility and changes in level of benefits, the VA projects an annual expenditure of over $9 billion for compensation and pension by 1990, an increase of 55 percent over 1971 outlays. The caseload will include 2.4 million veterans' and survivors' compensation cases and 2.6 million veterans' and

CHART 9

**THE COST OF COMPENSATION AND PENSIONS INCREASED 83 PERCENT
BETWEEN 1960 AND 1972**

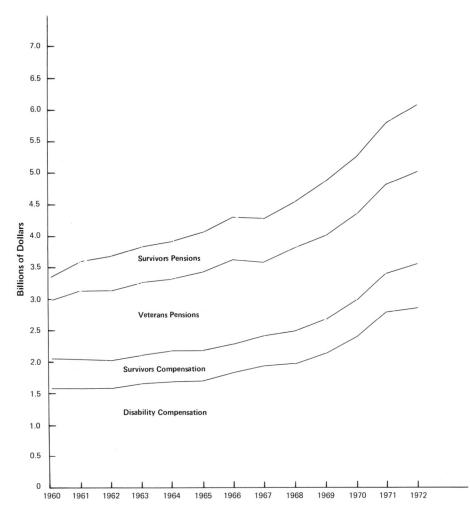

Source: Veterans Administration.

survivors' pension cases. At that time, the caseload and, consequently, the costs will presumably begin to taper off, assuming no new obligations or wars.

Compensation claims, traditionally established shortly after the end of each war, are expected to peak in 1976. War disabilities of Korean and Vietnam era wars will be established by that time for approximately 2.4 million claimants at an annual cost of $3.5 billion

(at the 1972 level of benefits). Compensation cases will start to decline
by 1976 due to higher mortality rates among the aging World War II
veterans, who compose about two-thirds of all compensation cases.
Thus deletions will exceed additions to the rolls. Compensation paid
to widows is expected to follow the same pattern, with the maximum
caseload of 387,000 cases occurring in 1976.

Pensions are expected to take a sharp upswing by 1976, reflecting
the advancing age of World War II veterans. The number of veterans
over 65 is expected to rise from 2 million in 1970 to 9.8 million in the
year 2000. The VA predicts that the upward trend in pension cases
will peak in 1990, with 2 million veterans and 2.6 million survivors
cases receiving $5.1 billion in pensions.[17]

While it may be a thankless task to question the validity of the
VA crystal ball, the assumptions on which the projections are based
are open to serious questions. The actual number of individuals who
will be pensioned in the future is a function of other universal income
support programs as well as the status of veterans' legislation. In 1971,
nearly four of every ten veterans aged 65 and older received pensions.
In that same year, close to 13 million of the surviving 14.3 million
World War II veterans were over 45 years old. By 1995, the number of
veterans over 65 years will rise from 2 million to over 9 million and if
the same proportion of World War II veterans should qualify for
pensions as veterans of World War I, this would yield close to 4 million
pensioners before the end of this century.

VA projections assume, however, that proportionately fewer aged
World War II veterans will be economically eligible for pensions because broader coverage of income security programs will reduce the
number of indigent aged veterans (table 16). However, despite more
comprehensive benefits provided through universal income support
programs, recent veterans' legislation continues to relax eligibility and

Table 16.   The VA Projects That a Decreasing Proportion of Aged
            Will Be Eligible for Pensions

	1970	1975	1980	1985	1990	1995
Veterans over 65 (thousands)	1,931	2,173	2,951	4,972	7,538	9,367
Percent with OASI Benefits	82	85	87	89	90	91
Veterans over 65 economically eligible for pensions (thousands)	1,587	1,493	1,524	1,710	1,791	1,442
Percent of Total	82	68	52	34	24	15

Source: U.S. Veterans Administration, Department of Veterans Benefits, *Estimated Demand and Cost for Pensions (1970–2000)*, December 1969, Tables 1, 3, and 5.

CHART 10

BARRING FUTURE WARS, COMPENSATION CASES WILL DECLINE BUT PENSION CASES WILL INCREASE UNTIL THE END OF THIS CENTURY

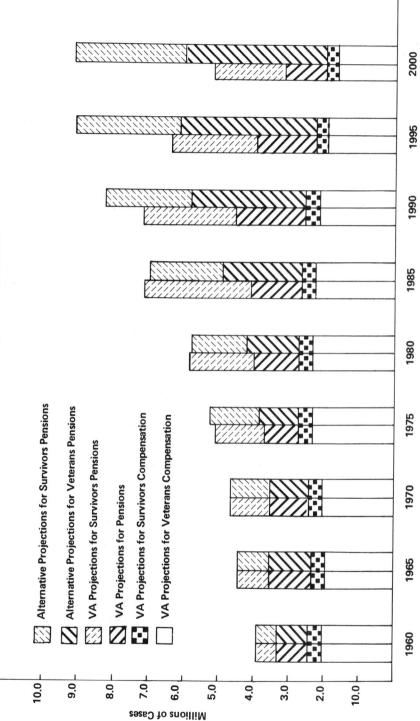

Legend:
- ▨ Alternative Projections for Survivors Pensions
- ▧ Alternative Projections for Veterans Pensions
- ▨ VA Projections for Survivors Pensions
- ▨ VA Projections for Pensions
- ▦ VA Projections for Survivors Compensation
- ☐ VA Projections for Veterans Compensation

Millions of Cases

Source: Veterans Administration.

boost benefits. It is quite clear that the VA projections tend to under-estimate significantly the likely eligibility and future cost of pensions. The agency assumed that Congress would hold qualifying income levels at the 1968 rate with increased social security and private pension cover-age limiting the number of eligible cases. However, since the VA released the projections, the qualifying income cut-off point has been raised 18 percent for veterans with one dependent and 30 percent for single veterans on pensions. In effect, Congress has not allowed termination of pensions due to increased social security benefits. This past per-formance indicates continued liberalization of benefit levels. If the same proportion of veterans and survivors remain eligible for pensions in future years, the pension caseload will continue to rise until the end of the century. At that time there would be 7.1 million veterans and survivors' pension cases, 28 percent more cases than the peak projected by the Veterans Administration for 1990 (chart 10). Rather than to assume that the income level of veterans qualifying for pensions will be frozen, it is more realistic to anticipate that future pension policies will continue to take into consideration the ever-rising income level of the American people and that the determination of veterans' needs will depend upon the relative affluence of the American people. If past experience is an indication of future developments, the rising levels of benefits will more than offset the declining number of compensation cases and pension recipients will continue to rise, perhaps at higher than expected rates. Also, the level of pensions will probably continue to rise. The actual costs of the veterans' compensation and pension programs will, therefore, far exceed official projections.

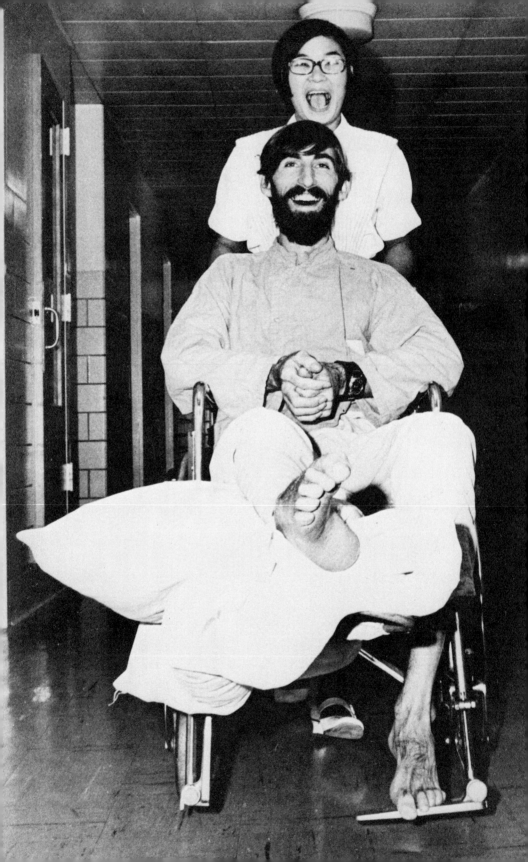

CHAPTER 3

Medical Care

To every thing there is a season,
and a time to every purpose under heaven:
A time to kill, and a time to heal;
a time to break down, and a time to build up.

Ecclesiastes 3:1–3

The VA Medical System

One of the tragedies of war is the damage inflicted upon the people who fight them. The injury to the victims cannot be undone, but the U.S. government has traditionally made all reasonable efforts to alleviate the suffering and to correct the damage. A primary mission of the Veterans Administration is to organize and deliver comprehensive care and rehabilitation to veterans who have incurred physical or psychological impairment in the course of military duty, and to care for medically "indigent" veterans, regardless of the cause of their affliction. While the rhetoric of Congress and the VA has emphasized care of war casualties, the trend has been to devote an increasing proportion of the medical resources to deliver health services for medically needy veterans whatever the source of their ailments.

The primary function of the Department of Medicine and Surgery, the health arm of the VA, is the delivery of medical care, but it has developed two related functions: providing clinical education and training to health care personnel, and funding medical research. The Veterans Administration justifies these programs in that they enhance the quality of veterans' health care by attracting teaching and research personnel.

In order to fulfill the mandate of delivering health care to veterans, the VA operates 167 hospitals, 75 nursing care units, and 18 domiciliaries. Ambulatory care is provided at 203 VA clinics. The VA also finances care obtained in private hospitals, nursing homes, state institutions, and in private physicians' offices. In addition to direct patient care, the VA finances about $188 million worth of education and research in various fields of medicine (table 17).

The 149,000 persons employed by the Department of Medicine and Surgery in 1972 accounted for 86 percent of the total VA staff, and constituted the largest complement of health care manpower em-

Table 17.   The VA Operated and Funded in 1972 a Broad Spectrum
             of Health Services

Activity	Cost (millions)	Staff (thousands)
Total Health Costs	$2,363.3	145.2
Medical Care	2,117.6	137.6
VA Operated		
Hospitals	1,571.2	113.4
Medical Beds	724.0	n.a.
Surgical Beds	414.0	n.a.
Psychiatric Beds	433.2	n.a.
Nursing Care	60.6	4.8
Domiciliaries	49.4	3.2
Outpatient Care	375.3	16.2
Contracted Facilities		
Hospitalization	19.7	—
Nursing Care	24.1	—
State Facilities	17.3	—
Education and Training	117.3	6.3
Research	70.3	.1
Miscellaneous	58.2	1.2

Source: Veterans Administration.
Note: Details may not add to totals because of rounding.

ployed in the United States by a single agency. Professional medical staff, including doctors, dentists, and nurses, are exempt from civil service hiring regulations and classifications. Paraprofessional and auxiliary personnel acquire permanent positions through the civil service system.

Two arguments have been advanced to justify the health care program. The first is society's responsibility to men incapacitated in service of the nation—a recognition of patriotism and sacrifice, even if it was involuntary. The second is the responsibility to provide health care to a segment of the elderly and indigent population on the grounds of past service to the country.

VA goes to considerable length to justify the expansion of medical care to the medically indigent. Agency spokesmen have claimed that the VA could not maintain the quality and comprehensiveness of its services if access were limited to service-connected cases. The VA contends that the array of ailments would be limited, the turnover of patients reduced, medical expertise would be narrowed, and VA hospitals would be an inadequate base for clinical teaching programs. This argument was somewhat compromised by the fact that even with the expanded eligibility for veterans, very few women and no children

were treated in VA hospitals, effectively limiting the type of case
load.

Aside from practical justification for care of nonservice-connected
cases, the VA argues it has a moral duty to care for the indigent who
have served the country. The VA slogan "to care for him who shall
have borne the battle" suggests a broad responsibility, with strong
overtones of sentimentality. In effect, the VA carries out eleemosynary
activities under a thin guise of "delayed compensation." Despite the
expanded federal responsibility for the delivery of health care to all
aged and indigent, there is every indication that Congress intends to
continue support for a parallel broadening of VA medical responsibilities, thereby maintaining a dual federally-supported medical program.
This is reflected not only in funding, which has doubled between 1960
and 1972, but also in the expansion of the VA's legislated responsibility
(chart 11). While the major factor accounting for the rise in VA medical outlays has been the 67 percent increase in the cost of medical care
between 1960 and 1972, the expansion of medical functions, including
medical research and education, nursing care, and ambulatory care
have also contributed to the rising health budget.

CHART 11

COSTS OF VA MEDICAL CARE MORE THAN DOUBLED BETWEEN 1960 AND 1972

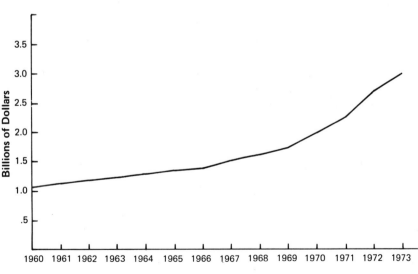

Source: Veterans Administration.

The VA expenditure in 1972 constituted about 2.7 percent of the $83 billion expended on health care in the United States. Federal outlays accounted for $21.6 billion and the total public expenditure on health equalled $32.8 billion (chart 12). The VA's medical budget in 1972 ranked third among federal health programs, behind Medicare expenditures for the elderly and Medicaid expenditures for the medically indigent.

The Organization of Health Care Delivery

The health care delivery systems operated by the federal government serve populations for whom the government has assumed special responsibility. Military personnel, American Indians, and federal prisoners are removed from typical health care facilities, and are, by law, wards of the state and thereby dependent upon federal medical aid.

CHART 12
SOURCES OF THE $83 BILLION NATIONAL HEALTH EXPENDITURE IN 1972

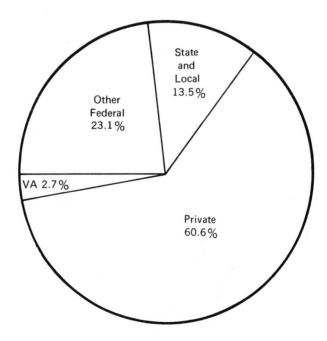

Source: Barbara S. Cooper and Nancy L. Worthington, "National Health Expenditures, 1929–72," Social Security Bulletin, January 1973, p. 7.

The medical care delivery system in the VA is exceptional in that it serves a broad population in the mainstream of American society. Most federal health care expenditures take the form of direct payments to vendors and the clients shop for services in the private sector. VA care, except for some service-connected cases, operates its own facilities which deliver complete care to clients.

Bureaucratic structure shapes the delivery of care. The Chief Medical Director "insures complete medical and hospital services for the medical care of veterans as prescribed by the administrator of Veterans Affairs pursuant to Title 38."[1] Five assistant chief medical directors oversee the separate major functions of planning and evaluation, administration and facilities, research and education, dentistry, and professional service. They are responsible for policy formulation and coordination in their respective areas.

Operational responsibility is delegated to four regional medical directors who serve as intermediaries between field station managers and central office staff in establishing and revising station missions. They collect and analyze operational data and monitor programs in their region to assure that overall VA policies and priorities are carried out.

Actual implementation of policies and delivery of care takes place at the individual hospital or domiciliary level. Hospital directors have leeway to adjust facility operations as long as they do so within budgetary constraints. Nonetheless, while a high degree of decentralization is encouraged, programs are monitored and coordinated by the central VA office.

Who Uses VA Hospitals?

Potentially, about 13 percent of the U.S. population is eligible to receive care. Perforce, the VA medical officials are selective in providing services. Veterans with access to hospital care include four identifiable overlapping groups: (1) veterans with service-connected disabilities; (2) recipients of veteran pensions; (3) veterans 65 years and older; and (4) medically "indigent" veterans. While the VA claimed that its health care system served six million of the 28 million veterans during 1971, only 760,000 of them were actually cared for in the VA hospitals.[2] Criteria governing eligibility for hospital care generally apply also to other VA health care benefits such as nursing care and outpatient treatment.

First priority to all VA health care goes to the two million men with service-connected disabilities—one of every fourteen veterans. These men place the greatest demands on the system. Veterans having total disability—nearly 127,000 veterans in 1972—are eligible for all medical services including ambulatory care for nonservice-connected conditions. Veterans are entitled to treatment of service-connected conditions no matter what the cost. A patient in a VA facility receives comprehensive care for all ailments regardless of the immediate cause for admission.

A patient with a service-connected disability is eligible for treatment of nonservice-connected conditions without signing a certification of need. Over half of the service-connected cases receiving hospital care in 1972 were admitted for treatment of an illness or malady which was not related to their service-connected condition (chart 13). This

CHART 13

MOST OF THE 776,000 VA HOSPITAL PATIENTS IN 1972 WERE TREATED FOR NONSERVICE-CONNECTED AILMENTS

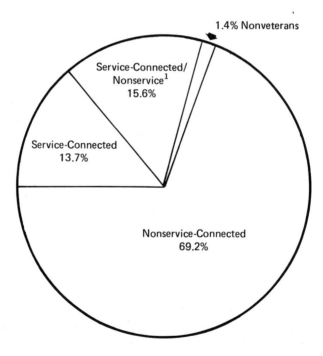

Source: Veterans Administration.

[1] Veterans with a compensable service-connected injury but treated for a nonservice-connected condition only.

privilege suggests additional compensation for the service-connected injury and also indicates that once the veteran becomes acquainted with the system he is more apt to return for care of other maladies.

Two-thirds of discharged hospital patients did not have a service-connected disability. Eligibility for hospital care is extended to "any veteran of any war or service after January 31, 1955 for a nonservice-connected disability if he is unable to defray the expenses of hospital care."[3] By law, veterans over 65 and veterans on pension are considered "unable to defray costs." Old age and poverty are frequent companions and one of every three veterans over 65 is on pension. In recognition of the high incidence of need among aged veterans and to avoid the stigma of means test, Congress removed in 1971 the certification of need requirement for veterans over 65. It is of special interest that Congress liberalized the admission of aged veterans to VA hospitals since Medicare, not to mention Medicaid, was already available to them. The availability of other "free" or insured medical care facilities has not appreciably reduced the demand for VA services. Hospital admission officers may still refer aged veterans to private care under Medicare, but records are not available on how frequently this happens. A study conducted in 1971 indicated that 74 percent of veterans with greatest entitlement to VA medical care—those on compensation and pension rolls—had some form of medical insurance.

Since the bulk of VA hospital patients qualify on the basis of need, it is not surprising that minority veterans are more than proportionately represented among the VA patients. Blacks constitute 8 percent of veterans but according to special surveys prepared by VA, close to 17 percent of VA patients in 1971 and 1972 were blacks.[4]

Of the 537,000 veteran hospital discharges in 1972 who had no service-connected disability, 36 percent were pensioners, and an additional 6 percent were not pensioned, but were over 65 years of age. The remaining 58 percent obtained care after certifying inability to defray costs. More than 3 of every 4 patients were below 65 years of age, suggesting that the vast potential clientele will continue to exercise strong pressures to maintain "free" VA hospitals (table 18).

A statement of "inability to defray costs" potentially opens VA medical care to most honorably or generally discharged veterans. Though the veteran is required to identify personal financial assets and to certify that he is medically indigent, the information submitted reflects the individual's opinion of what he can afford. If the veteran needs hospital care and has signed the required form, the VA is required to treat him or put him on a waiting list for treatment. The VA conducts pro forma counseling of applicants who may be able to afford other care and occasionally refers individuals suspected of supplying fraudulent information to the Department of Justice for

Table 18.   Three of Every Four Nonservice-Connected VA Patients
             Were below 65 Years of Age in 1972

(thousands)

Age	Total	Percent of Total	Pensioned	Percent of Total
All Ages	537.5	100.0	192.1	35.7
Under 34	77.7	14.5	2.1	.4
35–44	71.3	13.3	13.0	2.4
45–54	159.2	29.6	44.0	8.2
55–64	107.9	20.0	42.5	7.9
65 and over	121.3	22.6	90.5	16.8

Source: Veterans Administration.
Note: Details may not add to totals because of rounding.

prosecution. It shuns such action, however, and in 1971 it referred only three cases out of 1,310,574 applications to the Department of Justice. Clearly, the veteran population has rather easy access to VA medical facilities, especially if the illness constitutes a major medical expense.

Not all veterans eligible for VA care need or elect such hospitalization. A sample study of 1971 compensation and pension cases showed that 23 percent had been hospitalized within the year, of whom 69 percent had some hospitalization insurance. The majority of hospitalized veterans (61 percent) were treated in non-VA hospitals and 43 precent received care in VA hospitals (including 4 percent who were treated in both).

Half the pensioners and 39 percent of compensation cases who were hospitalized in VA facilities had health insurance. The fact that most health insurance plans, including Medicare, require partial payment and limit benefits makes VA care more attractive, especially to those on limited incomes. No data are available on the insurance status of VA patients who were neither compensation nor pension recipients.

VA hospital care may appeal to the veterans' pocketbook, but the system sacrifices certain amenities found in private hospitals. The patient cannot choose his physician and private facilities are rare. The comparison of VA facilities with the treatment offered patients in a charity ward is more flattering. On this basis, VA amenities, spartan as they may be, seem luxurious compared to some facilities available under Medicaid.

Hospital Facilities

The major components of the VA's health program consist of hospital care, ambulatory care, nursing home care, domiciliary and restoration care, education and training of health care manpower, and medical research. Hospital care has traditionally played the central role in VA medicine, taking a lion's share of the funds and medical personnel. The delivery of hospital care required 65 percent of VA medical care funds and employed 79 percent of VA health care personnel in 1971. During that year, VA hospitals accounted for 6 percent of all hospital beds in the United States:

Facilities	U.S. Total	VA Hospitals as Percent of Total
Hospitals	7,123	2.3
Beds	1,616,000	6.0
Average Daily Utilization	1,298,000	6.4

In 1972, the VA operated 167 hospitals containing 96,352 beds, 37,137 of which were designated for psychiatric care and 59,215 for general medical and surgical care. Each VA hospital treats both medical and psychiatric patients.

In addition to serving as dispensers of medical care, VA hospitals also serve as centers for clinical education and research. Medical specialization, location, and age of the facility determine the type of medical benefits delivered and the feasibility of supporting education and research projects. Some of the older VA hospitals are too remote to attract talented medical researchers. Acute care hospitals oriented toward nonpermanent medical conditions carry a larger range of specialized services and are usually located near a medical school with which they carry on cooperative clinical education programs. They are characterized by higher staffing ratios and more rapid patient turnover. An example of this is the 489-bed VA hospital at Durham, North Carolina. In 1970, the hospital employed 1.9 persons per patient and the monthly turnover of patients was 150 percent. The hospital is closely associated with Duke University medical school and provides clinical, internship, and residency training. The VA hospital at Salem, Virginia, is a contrast in hospital mission and orientation. The hospital is more isolated and is combined with a VA nursing home and domiciliary. In 1970, about one-third of the 604 beds were designated for intermediate or long-term care and the staff-to-patient ratio was 1:1.[5]

The 33 VA hospitals which care primarily for psychiatric patients are characterized by large physical plants, usually operating about 1,000 beds. Monthly turnover rates of patients are between 10 and 15 percent, reflecting slow recovery rates of persons afflicted with mental disorders. The staff-to-patient ratios are about 1:1 or less. An example is the facility at Danville, Illinois, which operated 1,553 beds in 1970.

The monthly patient turnover rate was 18 percent and the staffing ratio was 4:5.[6]

In addition to their medical orientation, the age of facilities influences the delivery of care. Aside from a few homes for disabled volunteer soldiers that date back to the nineteenth century, most hospital facilities were acquired immediately after World War I and World War II. Injured bodies and deserted military bases are the heritages of war and the Veterans Administration became the logical heir to surplus armed forces hospitals. However, remote base sites proved inadequate as hospital locations. Twenty-eight of the 62 hospitals acquired between 1919 and 1930 closed within the next three decades.[7]

Between 1930 and 1945, thirty hospitals were built, mostly in relatively isolated areas, and these hospitals care for a significant proportion of intermediate care patients.

World War II prompted another generous turnover of military hospital facilities and a renewed building program. Seventy-one facilities were acquired between 1946 and 1955, and 17 more were built by 1972. Although over 85 percent of VA facilities were constructed prior to 1950, the VA has carried on a continuous improvement program to update hospitals and add special services. Between 1960 and 1971, the VA expended $764 million on hospital construction and renovation.

VA facilities are spread throughout the country, as is the client population, but the selection of locations has changed in recent years. Prior to World War II, most VA facilities "were stuck," according to a former VA medical chief, "in far-off places, some of them on Indian Reservations, others as much as 50 miles from the nearest through-line railway stop."[8] After World War II, the VA policy was to locate new hospitals near medical schools and in large cities where adequate staffing could be acquired. More recently, Congress has encouraged states to build medical schools adjacent to VA hospital facilities in line with the recommendations of the Carnegie Commission Report on Higher Education and the Nation's Health.[9] Taking this trend one step farther, a 1972 bill authorized VA funding to help establish eight new medical schools.

Patient access and potential availability of staff are other major determining factors in locating hospitals. Presently, 90 percent of veterans live within 100 miles of a VA medical facility. Proximity to a hospital appears to affect utilization; the closer a veteran lives to a VA hospital facility, the more likely he is to use it. Veterans living within 25 miles of a facility account for over half of the VA hospital admissions, and more than two of every three patients live within 50 miles of the hospital site.[10]

Facility distribution is not strictly proportional to veteran population mostly because hospitals cannot be relocated to follow population movements. Population shifts have resulted in New York's 2.5 million veteran population being served by 11,000 hospital beds, while California's 3 million veterans are served by 9,000 beds. New construction sites in California and Florida are changing this imbalance, filling needs created by shifts of population to those states.

Psychiatric Care

Psychiatric care is traditionally long term and expensive. Although such care has been recognized and accepted as a public responsibility and a legal necessity, mental hospitals have not quite escaped their heritage of being state "prisons for the sick." Of the 506 psychiatric hospitals operating in 1969, state and local governments operated 284 facilities, encompassing 90 percent of all beds.[11] Publicly-financed institutions maintain occupancy rates between 85 and 90 percent due to high demand and slow turnover.

Although almost all VA hospitals operate some psychiatric-care beds, 72 percent of the VA's 44,000 psychiatric care beds in 1971 were in 33 predominantly psychiatric hospitals. Without these hospitals, most of the 38,000 psychiatric patients that the VA averaged in 1971 would have been shunted into financially hard-pressed and overcrowded state and local institutions.

Adequate financing, more staff, and availability of other medical care facilities allows the VA to provide psychiatric patients, in general, superior care to what is offered in many state and local institutions. Compared with other public psychiatric care institutions, the VA system maintains higher staff-to-patient ratios, 1:1 as opposed to 7:10 in state and local hospitals. On the average, VA hospitals also have somewhat faster turnover rates, since state and local institutions tend to have a more chronic caseload. The shorter stay in VA hospitals is also due to the VA's system of domiciliary facilities, which siphon off cases not requiring hospitalization. Many state institutions have no backup facilities for senile patients and other stabilized patients who require less attention than provided by hospitals. Also, veterans' compensation or pensions often provide financial ability for noninstitutionalized living. While the veteran is in the hospital he continues to receive his total compensation, but his pension is reduced after two full months of hospitalization to not more than $30 per month. If he has a dependent wife or child, the remainder of the pension may be paid to them.

The uncertainty of mental illness diagnosis and VA policy to give the patient the benefit of the doubt in judging medical need has led to higher acceptance rates of psychiatric than medical care applications.

Thirty-nine percent of persons who applied for VA medical care in 1970 were turned down because their conditions did not warrant hospitalization, but only 15 percent of psychiatric care applicants were not accepted.

The determination of service connection follows a different pattern in psychiatric cases than for other ailments. All active psychosis developed during service or within two years of discharge are considered service-connected, although some psychological instability or behavioral problems may have been latent previous to service, and only become apparent when particular behavior patterns were demanded and when combat stress was part of the job. Liberal assessment of service-connection and long-term institutionalization account for the fact that roughly half of hospitalized psychiatric patients are service-connected, while only 15 percent of general medical and surgical patients are receiving care for service-connected injuries. Psychiatric and neurological disabilities account for 21.9 percent of persons on VA compensation rolls.

Education, Training, and Research

Veterans Administration facilities offered clinical education and health training programs to over 53,000 persons at the cost of $103 million in 1971.[12] Educational institutions from medical schools to junior colleges and technical schools utilize VA facilities and staff for clinical internship and training to complement classroom work. These programs were originally limited to residency training, but now provide clinical training in practically every identifiable medical, laboratory, and hospital discipline.[13] Medical advances are introduced earlier and to a greater extent in teaching and research hospitals.[14] The VA's education programs have made new scientific developments available to VA teaching hospitals and placed them in a more advantageous position than many community hospitals.

The marriage of medical schools and VA hospitals is an arrangement under which the affiliated schools provide classroom training and the VA hospitals provide practical training grounds. The arrangement was initiated by General Paul R. Hawley and Dr. Paul B. Magnuson, directors of VA medical programs between 1945 and 1951. Prior to 1946, selection of VA doctors was subject to civil service regulations, a procedure with less than optimum results. A new practice initiated in 1946 exempted the appointment of doctors, dentists, and nurses from civil service regulations. This gave hospitals flexibility to bring in teaching doctors and residents. The "Dean's Committee," composed of senior faculty members of affiliated medical schools, select residents and medical chiefs, and evaluate residency programs in affiliated pro-

grams. Originally this program was designed to help man understaffed
VA hospitals, and to help young doctors discharged after World War
II to meet their residency training requirements. The cooperative
effort between schools and VA facilities was informal from 1946 until
1966, when it was given statutory recognition.

In 1971 a total of 82 medical schools were affiliated with 96 VA
hospitals. The cooperation between institutions has not only contributed to the medical manpower supply in VA hospitals, but also to
the national supply, since VA funds subsidize medical education. The
VA provides clinical facilities, teachers, and stipends to about 25 percent of residents participating in programs approved by the American
Medical Association and to about 50 percent of third and fourth year
medical students. The partnership is symbiotic. If separated, the VA
would suffer in the quality and quantity of its doctors and consultants,
while medical schools would be deprived of clinical facilities and supporting revenues for faculty salaries and stipends.

These generally profitable arrangements with medical schools have
generally maintained VA teaching hospitals on a par with university
hospitals, but difficulties have developed. First, the added costs have
strained VA resources, whose prime mission is to care for veterans.
Second, the VA clientele are not ideal for medical research. An acute-
care patient population with high turnover is optimum for teaching
situations. VA hospitals are mandated, however, to serve a population
which has excluded children and all but a few women. VA medical
officials are not free to select patients on the basis of their interest
for teaching or research purposes, though there has been some tendency
toward this practice. Thirdly, VA hospitals cannot maintain the 5:1
staff-to-patient ratio common to university hospitals, averaging 2:1 in
better VA hospitals. Evaluating VA hospitals, Dr. John A. D. Cooper,
president of the American Association of Medical Colleges, concluded
that VA care was good "compared with general care in the country . . .
but it is not up to the level of many academic medical centers."[15]

In addition to training physicians and dentists, the VA offers its
facilities to an array of academic disciplines and health training occupations which require clinical experience. In 1971, clinical training
was provided to about 15,600 prospective registered nurses. Other programs which handled fewer students included, among others, psy-
chology, social work clinical training, and technical training in occupational and physical therapy. The VA pays stipends only to residents
and interns, however, not to students.

VA facilities also host various non-VA, federally-funded man-
power programs, including institutional training under the Manpower
Development and Training Act, the Neighborhood Youth Corps, and
College Work-Study programs. The sponsoring agency provides in-

structors and pays trainees, while the VA supplies work stations and absorbs some overhead costs.

This long-standing commitment to training medical personnel has made the VA a vehicle for recent federal efforts to expand health care manpower. The Comprehensive Health Manpower Act of 1971 and the Nurse Training Act of 1971 were designed to meet the demand for health care manpower generated by Medicare, Medicaid, and expanded private demand. The VA will administer part of these new training efforts. VA's Department of Medicine and Surgery strongly favors the expansion of its educational and training activities and has urged that these activities be placed on an equal basis with its established mission of delivering medical care for veterans.[16]

Medical research, which was legislatively incorporated into the Department of Medicine and Surgery functions in 1958, is a complementary activity to the delivery of medical care to veterans and the support of education and training. In 1971, Congress appropriated $62 million to finance 5,283 research projects conducted in 136 VA institutions. In addition, VA funded investigators have also won grants from other funding sources. Research funds are an essential ingredient to the mutually rewarding affiliations between medical schools and VA hospitals. Medical school staff (and their students) who are also VA doctors may receive research grants from the VA. Availability of research funds adds to the amenities and attractiveness of the VA system for professional personnel.

Residential and Medical Care Outside Hospitals

The VA maintains a variety of residential and health care facilities to supplement hospital care and to provide residential facilities to indigent veterans. These facilities range from permanent residences provided for indigent and infirm veterans, to brief post-hospital care. In 1971, the price tag of these facilities was $94 million for 18,684 beds (table 19).

Domiciliaries and Restoration Centers

The earliest residential facilities were provided in the "National Asylums for Disabled Volunteer Soldiers." These domiciliaries were the veterans' version of poor homes and were among the first attempts by the federal government to provide for disabled or pauperized exsoldiers. The "soldiers' homes" maintained strong military overtones, and residents were subject to military law as if they were still on active duty.[17] These homes were put under the jurisdiction of the Veterans Administration upon its creation in 1930.

The VA has since discarded military overtones. Domiciliaries have

Table 19. In 1971 the VA Provided a Broad Spectrum of Residential
Medical Care outside Hospital Settings

Type of Facility	Number of Beds	Total Patients Treated	Daily Cost per Patient	Cost per Patient
VA facilities				
Nursing care	5,052	7,389	$27	$6,193
Domiciliaries	12,873	25,666	10	1,702
Restoration Centers	759	2,467	17	1,679
Non-VA facilities				
Community nursing care	—	12,803	16	1,505
State home nursing care	—	5,413	5	966
State domiciliaries	—	11,129	3.50	664
State home hospitals	—	6,728	7.50	434

Source: U.S. Veterans Administration, *Medical and Construction Appropriations and Funds,* Congressional Submission, vol. 3, fiscal year 1973, pp. 2–13 and 2–14.

become refuge centers which "provide care on an ambulatory self-care basis for veterans disabled by age or disease who are not in need of acute hospitalization and who do not need the skilled nursing services provided in a nursing home."[18] Residents of domiciliaries need only minimum supervision and care, but are unable to function outside a sheltered environment.

Initially, eligibility was restricted to veterans separated from active duty for disabilities, or to disability compensation recipients who suffer from permanent disabilities which incapacitate them from earning a living and who have no adequate means of support. A 1966 law extended eligibility to all who needed domiciliary care and could not afford it. Direct applications accounted for more than half of the admissions to domiciliary facilities in 1970. Other routes of access into VA domiciliaries include referral from other VA facilities, especially psychiatric hospitals.

According to a 1961 study, most of the residents were in their late 50s and 60s. About three in ten persons had some service-connected disability, but that was not the primary cause for seeking domiciliation. Members tended to have little education—over 50 percent had reached only the 8th grade—and social adjustment problems. They were social dropouts and their work records tended to be unsteady and marginal.[19] Forty percent of domiciliary members have had alcoholic problems and suffer from the psychiatric or physical debility which accompanies long-term alcoholic excess. Many have clashed with the law and have spent time in jail.[20]

A more recent trend has been placement of long-term psychiatric patients in domiciliaries where they are sheltered, but live relatively more independent lives. Individuals are encouraged to assume responsibilities that range from minimal self-care to work incentive programs in which individuals earn salaries for services rendered.

In 1971, the VA operated 16 domiciliaries with a bed capacity of almost 13,000 and an average daily occupancy of 12,000 persons. Of 1971 discharges, the average stay was 361 days. Over half of newly-admitted members had been domiciled previously, which would suggest that the total time spent in domiciliaries is usually even longer.

In addition to supporting a daily average of 12,000 patients in VA domiciliaries, in 1971 grants-in-aid were extended to states to help defray the cost of domiciling veterans in state institutions. In the case of state domiciliaries, administration and admission policy are left to the states. The VA subsidizes the states at $3.50 a day, or one-half per diem costs, whichever is less, if the institutionalized individual would have otherwise been eligible for admission to a VA domicile.

Restoration centers represented a short-lived attempt to prepare domiciled veterans for return to community life. Candidates with potential for independent living were selected for rehabilitation therapy and counseling to help them cope with their problems. Community facilities for educational advancement, and job training and placement, including MDTA programs and state employment agencies, were used in preparing these men for noninstitutionalized life. As of July 1, 1972, the program was discontinued without a formal justification. It may be guessed that the project was considered a failure.

Nursing Care—An Expansion of Hospital Care

The function of nursing home care is to provide appropriate care to hospitalized individuals who are not yet ready for ambulatory care, but who no longer require hospitalization. Formerly, the VA maintained "intermediate" care hospital beds because provision of separate nursing care was not authorized. In the early 1960s chronically ill patients occupied over 60 percent of VA hospital beds, causing slow turnover. To "unfreeze" these beds, the VA began in 1965 to operate nursing care units and to contract for care in private facilities as well as to subsidize care of veterans in state nursing homes. From a modest beginning, the nursing care programs were expanded by 1972 to provide services to almost 13,000 veterans (chart 14). The scope of the program is expanding. The limit on VA nursing beds was raised from 4,000 to 6,000, by a 1970 executive order, and 1972 legislation boosted the limit to 8,000 beds.

Apart from federal facilities, 22 states support a total of 27 nursing homes for veterans. Admission to and regulation of the facilities are state functions. But individuals who would have otherwise been eligible for VA care are partially supported by the VA in a fifty-fifty cost

CHART 14

**AVERAGE DAILY PATIENTS IN NURSING CARE INCREASED STEADILY
BETWEEN 1965 AND 1972**

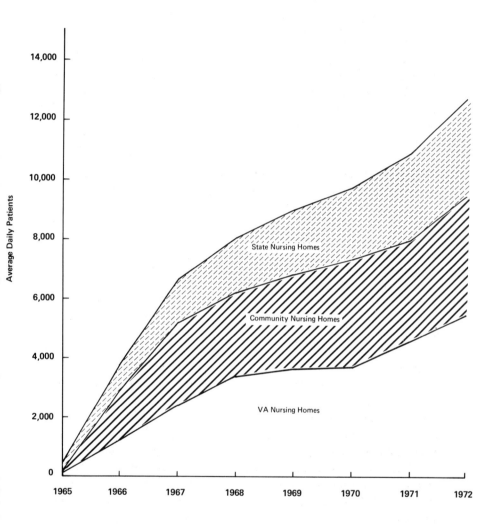

Source: Veterans Administration.

agreement with the states. In 1972, the VA helped maintain 3,200 patients at the average daily cost of $5.00 per patient. The average patient stay was about two years. Judged by the outlays, life in a state nursing home is a rather meager existence.

Under a 1964 law, the federal government extended an annual matching grant of $5 million to states for construction of more state nursing care beds. The VA pays 50 percent of costs as long as the supply of beds does not exceed 1.5 per 1,000 veterans. Only $16.0 million of the $18.5 million appropriated in the first five years of the program has been committed to states, because funds were partially impounded by the Office of Management and Budget. All in all, about 2,300 beds have been added to state systems through this program.

When VA nursing care was initiated in 1965, the Bureau of the Budget directed that unused hospital beds be converted for nursing care. The budget bureau's logic was impeccable, but the unused beds were not located where they were needed. They were not in centrally located acute-care hospitals which needed them, but in psychiatric hospitals and in peripherally located hospitals.

This mislocation of VA nursing care beds resulted in operational difficulties for acute-care hospitals which needed nursing facilities for patients who no longer required hospitalization but still required some care. Geographic distances and the attempt to maintain a desired "mix" of severe and less severe cases caused a backlog of patients waiting for nursing care. To overcome locational mismatch, the VA acquired extra facilities through contracts with community facilities. Community nursing care beds are procured by each hospital according to need, provided the cost is less than 40 percent of VA hospitalization. The cost limitation creates problems in high cost areas such as New York City, where fees are in excess of VA maximum payments for nursing care.

Individual hospitals maintain varying numbers of patients in community facilities depending on the pressure for hospital beds. The law specifies that an individual may be maintained in community nursing facilities at VA expense for up to six months but, as usual, exceptions may be made, especially for service-connected cases. In 1971, the average cost per patient episode in community facilities came to $1,505, and the average stay lasted about three months.

Since the VA expanded its operations into nursing care, the daily hospital utilization has dropped from 109,000 patients in 1965 to 81,000 in 1972. It is possible that nearly half of this drop in hospital utilization may have been due to the availability of nursing care. However, the expansion of VA nursing care coincided with the initiation of Medicare and Medicaid programs, and undoubtedly the alternative programs have also had some effect in lowering VA hospital use. Since the passage of Medicare and Medicaid in 1965, the total number of patients discharged from VA hospitals rose from 611,000 to 776,000 but the number of patients aged 65 and over declined from 207,000 to 147,000. This lower utilization by the aged was only partly explained by a 10 percent decline in the total number of aged veterans. It is probable that both Medicare and VA nursing care both contributed to the lower daily usage of VA hospitals.

Outpatient Clinics

Outpatient clinics provide three main services: (1) ambulatory care to veterans with service-connected disabilities; (2) medical evaluations for VA hospitalization, domiciliation, or other benefits; and (3) follow-up care to persons hospitalized in the VA system. Ambulatory care has been expanded recently to permit veterans with nonservice-connected ailments to get outpatient treatment in conjunction with VA hospitalization.

The VA operates 203 outpatient clinics, mostly located in the 167 VA hospitals. In 1971, the agency recorded more than 8 million medical visits and nearly half a million dental examinations at a cost of $302 million. Nearly a fifth of this amount was used to reimburse 1.5 million contracted or "fee" medical and dental visits (table 20).

Table 20.   The VA Expended $302 Million for Outpatient Care in 1971

Type of Care	Outlays (millions)	VA Facilities		Contracted Services	
		Number of visits (thousands)	Units Cost	Number of Contracted Visits (thousands)	Units Cost
Total	$302.3	6,476	—	1,517	—
Total Medical Care	186.8	6,245	—	1,258	—
Service-connected	61.3	2,648	$ 18	1,169	$ 11
Nonservice-connected	24.6	1,595	15	—	—
Compensation & Pension	14.9	370	37	86	15
Insurance Exams	.4	9	38	1	10
Hospital & Domiciliary Care	15.7	1,371	11	2	8
Prehospital Care	2.4	114	21	—	—
Day Hospital	1.4	45	31	—	—
Trial Visits	2.4	93	26	—	—
Prosthetics	23.5	—	—	—	—
Prescriptions	20.8	—	3	—	8
Other Outpatient	19.4	—	—	—	—
		Completed Cases			
Dental Care	55.3	231	—	259	—
Exams	5.1	148	15	98	29
Treatments	50.2	83	103	161	259
Support Cost	60.2	—	—	—	—

Source: U.S. Veterans Administration, Office of the Controller, "Outpatient Care— Direct Costs," Table 1.

The law specifies that outpatient medical services, defined as medical examinations and treatment, prosthetic devises, and optometrist, dental, and surgical services, may be furnished for treatment of service-connected disabilities. Outpatient medical service under contract is still largely limited to service-connected cases. But as with other medical care, many nonservice-connected cases are treated in VA clinic facilities.

Nearly a third of the service-connected visits were handled through the "Hometown Medical Program" which allows service-connected disabilities to be treated by private physicians with the VA picking up the tab. Fee basis outpatient care is authorized for service-connected cases when the patient requires specific treatment which is unavailable at the VA clinic, when demand for service exceeds the capacity of VA clinics, or when travel to clinics places undue hardship on the patient. Many service-connected patients are too distantly located to use VA clinics conveniently.

Outpatient medical services also include a variety of rehabilitation services. Speech and audiology therapy, rehabilitation for the blind, and treatment of drug addiction and alcoholism are given in clinics as well as in hospital settings. Mental hygiene clinics provide psychiatric care and counseling.

Dental Care

Large scale dental care is a recent addition to the VA package of medical services, and is predominantly limited to service-connected conditions. Every veteran is entitled to one complete dental treatment if he applies within one year after separation from service. The assumption is that dental care needed within that year had its origins in the service. Some needy veterans have also become eligible for dental treatment since the VA ministers to all dental needs of all patients in VA hospitals, nursing homes, or domiciliaries. The cost of dental care is mounting and has reached $55.3 million in 1971, a fivefold rise in the cost of the program in three years.

Provisions for dental care are liberal and liberally used—especially by recently discharged veterans. According to one VA official, the Department of Defense has been lax in providing dental care, anticipating that the VA will correct the deficiency after discharge from the armed forces. Most of the dental patients in recent years have been Vietnam veterans. Applications have increased fourfold between 1967 and 1971. The VA received 302,000 applications for dental care and accepted 262,000 cases for treatment, virtually all of whom were Vietnam era veterans.

The accelerated demand for dental care has overtaxed VA facilities and the agency has relied increasingly on contracted services. Over 85 percent of treatments in 1967 were handled by VA staff. Four years later private dentists provided two-thirds of all treatments. The increased reliance on non-VA dentists to relieve the backlog required the VA to allocate $31 million of the $105 million 1971 supplemental appropriation to pay for contracted dental care.

The dental program is the second most expensive ambulatory care program, surpassed only by medical treatment of service-connected cases. Costs per patient under contract averaged $29 for an examination and $259 for complete dental treatment. Evidently, many servicemen leave the military without receiving the corrective dental care they should, shifting the responsibility later to the VA at an annual cost of $50 million. Nonetheless, considering that most patients were youthful veterans, the presumed deteriorated dental conditions as reflected by the high costs per patient must be a cause of concern to American health authorities, not to mention the taxpayer who foots the bill.

A Funnel for Access

Outpatient facilities are the gateway to establishing medical eligibility for various VA benefits. Compensation cases must be rated to determine the degree of physical damage or psychological impairment that has been incurred. Also, to qualify for pensions prior to their 65th birthday, veterans must be found to be permanently disabled, as well as needy. Most of these determinations are made in VA facilities, but nearly a fifth of the 456,000 compensation and pension applications that required medical examination in 1971 were handled by private physicians. Private doctors charged the VA $15 per visit in 1971, less than half of the estimated cost to VA of handling a visit in its own clinics.

Applications for VA hospital services have risen by more than 30 percent between 1968 and 1971. Examinations to determine medical justification for hospitalization or domiciliation for service and non-service-connected cases accounted for 1,373,000 visits in 1971. About 40 percent of hospital care applicants were found ineligible because their conditions did not warrant hospitalization and about one-third of those denied admission received some treatment on the spot despite the fact that the law does not provide for "medical services" for non-service-connected cases.[21]

Another outpatient activity is conducted in connection with the widespread VA insurance operations. The law stipulates that premium payments on National Life Insurance policies may be waived if the insured veteran is totally disabled for six or more months. In order to obtain the waiver, an individual must submit to medical examinations to determine disability and must allow reexamination to verify the continuation of the disability. Also, individuals who have allowed their insurance to lapse for more than six months and who desire reinstatement must provide proof of good health established by a complete physical examination. Some 10,000 such examinations were given in 1971.

A Supplement to Hospital Care

Outpatient clinics not only provide access to hospital care but also help speed the release of hospital patients. Programs initiated in 1960 allow outpatient clinics to provide "medical services" to veterans with nonservice-connected conditions prior to or after hospitalization. Facilities for posthospital care allow physicians to hospitalize patients for a short time, and then follow up with ambulatory care for an indefinite period.

Prehospitalization care is usually limited to patients who are near to the hospital or those with less serious conditions. Posthospital care is more broadly used. It accounted for 1.6 million visits in 1971 at $15 per visit, for a total cost of $24.6 million. Supplementary outpatient care has shortened hospital stays and helped use inpatient facilities efficiently. Greater turnover of patients allows more patients to be treated, and generally upgrades hospital service by providing more appropriate care. Follow-up care is used in psychiatric as well as medical cases.

Three outpatient programs are designed specifically for psychiatric and neurological treatment. These are trial visits, day treatment centers, and day hospital care. The trial visits program was designed to sidestep the pre-1960 ban on outpatient care for nonservice-connected cases. Nonservice-connected cases released from psychiatric hospitals had to acquire follow-up care through private physicians. Most of the discharged patients were indigent and few had their own physicians. Without follow-up support, many headed right back to the hospital. The trial visits program placed patients back into their communities while officially keeping them on hospital rolls. In this way, VA personnel could monitor patient programs and provide additional care when needed. Since posthospital care is now officially provided, the rationale for trial visits has been eliminated and the program is being phased out.

Day hospitals and day treatment centers are specialized medical services delivering psychiatric care and counseling on an outpatient basis. Day treatment centers, in operation since 1958, work in conjunction with VA mental health clinics to rehabilitate chronic psychiatric patients. Under this program the VA operated 38 facilities in urban areas in 1971. Patients come on a daily basis for group therapy sessions and work training with the objective of eventual independent living.

Day hospitals provide intensive psychiatric care to veterans suffering from acute anxiety and other psychological conditions without uprooting them from home and community. The program is designed to obviate the need for hospitalization and is available for service-connected and nonservice-connected conditions. In operation since 1964, the program operated 16 centers in 1971, providing 45,000 visits at an average cost of $31.00 per visit, about equal to the average daily cost of care in a VA psychiatric hospital. The VA claimed that day hospital programs effected substantial economic savings and maintained that each session saved 28.6 days of care in a psychiatric hospital. Consequently, the VA has favored expanding day hospital programs. Optimistic VA officials anticipate that broader use of the day hospital program will result in declining unit costs made possible by economies of size.

A related effort to reduce extended stays in hospitals was initiated in 1972 by the home care pilot project.[22] Under this program, patients are discharged to their homes. A caretaker, usually the patient's wife or some other family member, is trained by the VA staff in the patient's dietary and other needs. The community visiting nurses association makes home calls and assists the caretaker, as does a VA social worker. VA physicians conduct routine house calls and emergency visits if the need arises.

This program could effect considerable savings over institutionalized care by making use of VA and community medical resources. Potential recipients of such care are limited to persons who have stable homes and family members who fit the caretaker role. As additional qualifications, these homes must be located in the vicinity of a VA hospital, and supporting medical services must be available in the community.

Alcoholic and Drug-dependent Veterans

"Drinking," John Dryden wrote nearly three centuries ago, "is the soldier's pleasure," and VA hospitals can testify that the maxim is still true. Alcohol problems are part of the medical diagnosis for one of every six VA hospital patients. Alcoholic veterans are accepted for treatment in the same manner as those requesting care for any other medical condition. The director of the VA Drug and Alcohol Dependence Service estimated that three million veterans suffered from alcoholism in 1971, the highest incidence occurring among middle-aged veterans.[23]

The VA initiated a special medical program with separate funding for alcohol-dependent veterans in 1969. Emphasis was placed on rehabilitation of the individual as well as treatment of associated medical problems. By 1972, the VA operated 41 alcohol treatment units with a total of 1,500 beds and an annual cost of $13.2 million, and plans had been made to extend the service.

Alcoholism affects twenty times as many veterans as other kinds of drug dependence. Long term alcohol abuse inflicts greater physical damage and more severe withdrawal reactions than does heroin addiction. However, alcohol abuse and its treatment have not generated nearly the controversy that drug use and rehabilitation have stirred up.

The VA has extended specialized treatment to alcoholic veterans for some time, despite the fact that alcoholism is a nonservice-connected disability. Recent concern for drug-dependent veterans has posed more problems not only for the VA, but also for the military in the identification and rehabilitation of durg users. Moreover, the classification of drug dependence among veterans as a purely societal problem is inconsistent with evidence that drug abuse among veterans may be service-connected, if not service-induced. The General Accounting Office found, for example, that drugs have been readily and cheaply available to servicemen in Vietnam.[24]

Veterans who were interviewed by Louis Harris noted that personal problems, boredom, and military life encouraged drug abuse among servicemen. Whatever the reason for drug use among military personnel, the proportion of those who used drugs while in the military was almost double the percentage who had experimented with drugs in civilian life. The study observed that "it would be a legitimate conclusion to call the military a breeder of drug use."[25]

Estimates of the extent of drug use among servicemen and veterans vary widely. Dr. Jerome Jaffe, director of the Special Action Office for Drug Abuse Prevention (SAODAP), reported that between 4 and 5 percent of those soldiers screened by urinalysis tests showed postive results. Louis Harris reported that only 2 percent of Vietnam veterans were heroin addicts upon their return to civilian life. While SAODAP estimated that in 1972 there were approximately 100,000 addicted veterans of all ages among the 500,000 to 750,000 drug-addicted Americans, the VA estimated the number at 60,000 veterans.[26]

The VA has extended the classification "service-connected disability" to veneral disease, but drug abuse and alcoholism remain nonservice-connected. If either were to become compensable, the VA would be required to provide not only hospitalization and compensation, but also vocational rehabilitation services to those affected. Instead, the VA has unofficially treated the veteran addict as a special case and provided him services not actually required by law, and not generally available to veterans with nonservice-connected medical problems. While most veterans must meet a nominal needs test to be eligible for VA treatment, veteran addicts are generally admitted for drug treatment with little regard to financial need. Proposals that VA drug treatment be made available to veterans regardless of their discharge status have been opposed as inequitable by the VA and the veterans' lobby, since veterans discharged under less than honorable conditions are excluded from VA care, even if they have a service-connected disability.

To help extend the VA services to those with other than honorable discharges, in August 1971 the Secretary of Defense ordered that discharges solely for drug offenses be reviewed upon request of the veteran and changed to administrative discharges "under honorable conditions." While administrative discharges for drug abuse rose from 5,000 to 9,000 between 1970 and 1971, the proportion of undesirable discharges solely for drug usage fell as the armed services began "exemption programs" during mid-1971 for drug abusers who voluntarily requested assistance. Under these programs men could ask for medical help for their drug problems without risking court-martial or discharge under less than honorable conditions. The GAO reported that the success of the program is limited because soldiers who use drugs and the Department of Defense distrusted each other.[27]

During 1971 over 16,000 drug abusers voluntarily asked for treatment under the exemption programs; 9,000 other drug users were identified through law enforcement activities. In June 1971, urinalysis testing for servicemen in Vietnam began. When a soldier is identified as a drug user, he is normally sent to an armed services detoxification center for 3 to 14 days and some are referred to VA drug treatment facilities for continued assistance.[28]

The VA opened the first Drug Dependence Treatment Center in January 1971, and operated 44 centers eighteen months later. Over 11,000 veterans were admitted to VA facilities with drug-dependence problems during 1971; another 8,800 veterans and 2,700 servicemen were admitted to such facilities during the first six months of 1972. The eventual cost per veteran for a full three years of treatment was projected at $4,750.[29]

Four of every ten drug patients continued with outpatient treatment upon discharge from the VA hospitals. Of the 6,000 veterans who left outpatient care between January 1971 and June 1972, 1,900 were rehospitalized and 1,600 terminated the program. While the latter number is probably the most accurate estimate of those who successfully completed treatment, the rehabilitation criteria for the drug dependent veteran are not well defined. In light of the VA's original estimate that a successful rehabilitation program would require three to six weeks of hospitalization and then approximately 70 outpatient visits each year for as long as three years, it may be assumed that a significant proportion of drug patients leave the program prior to successful rehabilitation.

Administrator Donald Johnson noted that satisfactory job placement would be one measure of successful rehabilitation for the addict. The VA has arranged for at least one vocational counselor to be assigned to each of the drug treatment facilities to aid drug abusers in making the transition from medical care to school, training, or employment. However, the VA has opposed legislation that would formally extend its vocational rehabilitation program to veteran addicts. Instead, the drug program relies on medical care for the drug dependent veteran, combined with education and training under the regular GI bill as if the veteran had experienced no disabling problem.

Alternative Options

Two other major federal health programs, Medicare and Medicaid, parallel the VA health delivery system by serving the elderly and the medically indigent. Medicare accounts for the largest block of federal funds, and is administered through established insurance companies, Blue Cross being the major intermediary. Medicare is based on the insurance practice of spreading the cost risk of illness and the federal government exercises little regulation of the health care delivered. Medicaid monies are matched by the states and are filtered through their welfare departments. States pay the physician or facility providing the medical care.

It might have been anticipated that the passage of Medicare and Medicaid would reduce the demand for VA hospitalization care. In fact the number of veterans treated annually has continued to rise. And rather than to reduce the duplication of hospital coverage for the aged and needy, Congress has continued to expand VA health care benefits. Five years after Medicare and Medicaid were placed on the law books, Congress made veterans over 65 eligible to obtain VA hospitalization without signing a certification of need. Men over 65 accounted for about 18 percent of nonservice-connected VA hospital discharges in 1971.

From 1968 to 1971, demand for VA hospital services jumped 30 percent. Partly, this increase reflected greater use of health care facilities throughout American society. Rising medical costs, even with medical insurance, prompted more veterans to seek VA medical care. The elderly living on fixed incomes and young Vietnam veterans who either could not find jobs or who have not yet established themselves in jobs and therefore had no work-related health insurance, were especially likely to make use of VA care. Whether demand for VA medical care will become an established practice for these veterans will depend upon their future economic fortunes and the ease with which these services can be obtained. Unless substantial changes are made in the alternative public health programs, it is likely that greater and greater numbers will turn to the VA for medical care.

While Medicare may have blunted most of the economic sting of serious illness, the remaining financial burdens are still significant. Medicare covers up to 90 days of hospital care for each "benefits period," but the individual must pay the first $68 and an additional $17 a day after 60 days of care. The average hospital bill per Medicare patient in 1971 was $1,133, of which government insurance covered only 77 percent. This left the patient with an out-of-pocket cost of $261, which may be a considerable financial burden to the aged patient living on a limited income with little room for "extras." In contrast, the VA hospitalization is completely free to veterans.

Medicaid, the health care program for "medically indigent" under the general welfare system, is administered by the states under federal guidelines. As with other public assistance programs, medical assistance is subject to variations in eligibility criteria according to state policy. In 25 states, eligibility for medical vendor payments is restricted to welfare recipients. In the states where Medicaid is extended to persons not on public assistance, annual income limitations for a single person ranges from $1,100 in Oklahoma to $2,500 in Connecticut and Rhode Island. In addition to income limitations, cash and other liquid resources are usually limited to $1,500 or less. Little consideration is therefore given to the depletion of the patient's resources, since virtually everyone who qualifies has precious little to begin with.

Compare this approach with the treatment offered by the VA. Almost half the individuals treated in VA hospitals receive care under a claim of medical indigency. However, the criteria for indigency are much more lenient. Middle-income veterans (the median annual income of American families in 1971 was $10,285) may qualify for costly medical treatment (of a kidney malfunction, for instance) if the appropriate VA officials believe that the medical bill would deplete the financial resources of the veterans. Under this definition, only affluent families could bear the costs of catastrophic illness without becoming "medically indigent."

The VA does not demand abject poverty before it extends its medical benefits. Eligibility it flexible and subjective, thus eliminating the income notch problem which plagues most public assistance programs. If a veteran's income rises a few dollars it will not disqualify him from VA care, while a small increase in income can change the eligibility status of welfare recipients.

The comparison of VA medical care with other public health care is not entirely in the VA's favor. A Medicaid recipient is entitled to basic medical services, including inpatient hospital care, outpatient hospital service, other laboratory and X-ray services, and a physician's services. Medicaid pays for office visits and allows the individual to receive care for conditions which do not warrant hospitalization. VA care for nonservice-connected care is restricted. Medicaid recipients have freedom to choose their physicians. Beneficiaries of VA medical care do not have a choice of medical vendor.

Although the location of doctors' offices and hospitals and limited mobility among the poor tend to curtail the individual's choice of physicians, the opportunity to seek and choose medical help generally allows Medicaid recipients greater access to care than some veterans enjoy. VA hospital locations favor veterans in areas where the facilities are located and tend to leave out veterans with no nearby facility. On balance, for veterans with an accessible facility, and little money for medical care, the process of obtaining free care from the VA is more humane and dignified than the public assistance or public hospital route.

Cost and Efficiency of VA Medical Care

The costs of VA hospital care have experienced the same inflation which has hit private sector hospitals (chart 15). Costs per patient day have rocketed because of rising wages of hospital personnel, a traditionally underpaid group; failure of the supply of medical health care personnel to keep up with rising demand; the slow growth in output per unit of labor; and new technological innovations requiring large investments in equipment and high operational expenditures. VA hospitals compete for personnel and have to provide comparable salaries and benefits; and VA teaching hospitals must keep up with medical innovations in order to maintain quality care and education.

The per diem cost of care in community hospitals during the past decade has been one and one-half times as much as that for VA general hospitals. Relatively higher per diem costs in community hospitals are primarily due to higher staffing ratios and a greater percent of acute care patients. In 1971, private community hospitals maintained 3:1 average staff-to-patient ratio, compared with 8:5 for VA medical and surgical facilities.[30] An additional factor adding to per diem expense in private hospital care is duplication of facilities, resulting in inefficient utilization. Private hospitals serve as community status symbols and the federal construction subsidies supplied by the Hill-Burton Act have resulted in overproduction of hospital beds. Duplication of spe-

CHART 15

COSTS OF HOSPITAL CARE HAVE RISEN STEADILY IN BOTH VA AND COMMUNITY HOSPITALS OVER THE LAST DECADE

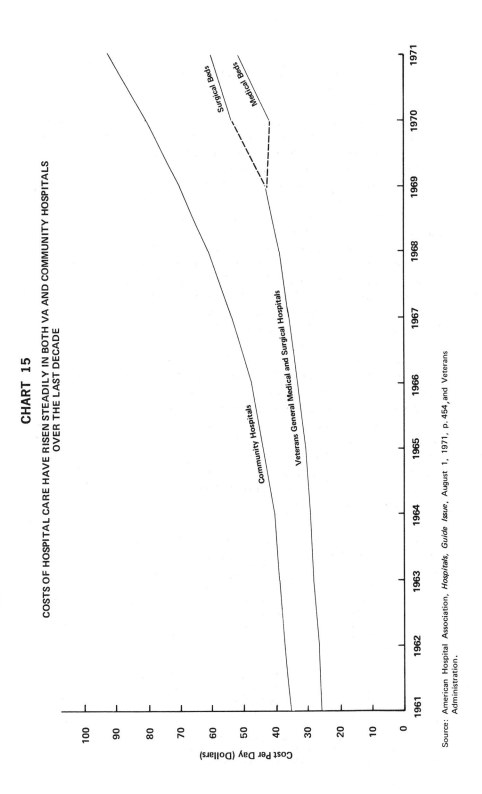

Source: American Hospital Association, *Hospitals, Guide Issue*, August 1, 1971, p. 454, and Veterans Administration.

cial treatment facilities, such as cobalt bombs, have also resulted in costly underutilization.

Also, hospitals have the ability to shift increased costs onto the consumer without facing a consumer revolt. The ill patient may not be in a position to haggle over prices. Moreover, the growth of medical insurance creates the illusion that a third party pays the bill, and this has blunted pressure to hold down costs, although more recently the inevitable boosts in insurance rates have stimulated outcries against rising medical costs.

The savings generated by the VA's efficient use of personnel and facilities are lost, however, because patient turnover rates are appreciably lower than in community hospitals. The cost per patient treated in VA hospitals exceeds comparable costs in community hospitals because patients remain longer in VA hospitals. The average length of stay in community hospitals has fluctuated between seven and nine days over the last 25 years.[31] In comparison, the average length of stay for VA medical and surgical cases was 23.2 days in 1972, a drop from 30.5 days seven years earlier (table 21). The average length of stay in VA hospitals is exaggerated by a small percentage of patients who are hospitalized for inordinately long stays. In 1972 the majority of patients were hospitalized less than 14 days (chart 16).

Several factors contribute to the relatively slower turnover rate in Veterans Administration hospitals. First, older patients tend to stay in hospitals longer than younger people. While individuals over 65 accounted for about twenty percent of hospital discharges from both community and VA hospitals, VA hospital patients are all adults and preponderently middle-aged and older men, and community hospitals serve the entire population. But age alone does not explain the longer

Table 21.   The Patient Stays Three Times Longer in General Medical and Surgical VA Hospitals than in Community Hospitals

	Average Length of Stay	
Year	VA Hospitals	Community Hospitals
1965	30.5 days	7.8 days
1966	30.4 days	8.0 days
1967	28.7 days	8.3 days
1968	27.8 days	8.5 days
1969	26.5 days	8.4 days
1970	25.0 days	8.3 days
1971	24.4 days	n.a.
1972	23.2 days	n.a.

Source: U.S. Congress, House Appropriations Committee, HUD-Space-Science Appropriations for 1973, 92nd Cong., 2nd sess., 1972, p. 592; and Julian H. Pettengill, "Trends in Hospital Use by the Aged," Social Security Bulletin, July 1972, p. 13.

CHART 16

THE MAJORITY OF VA MEDICAL AND SURGICAL PATIENTS WERE HOSPITALIZED LESS THAN FOURTEEN DAYS IN 1972

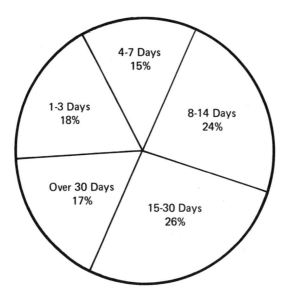

Source: Veterans Administration.

stay in VA hospitals. Medicare patients spent an average of 12.4 days in hospitals in 1971, compared with the 33.4 days average stay of patients aged 65 and older in VA hospitals.[32]

Second, the VA treats multiple conditions in one admission and releases the patient after delivering "maximum hospital benefits." According to one study, probably much of this treatment could be delivered more cheaply outside the hospital, as it is in the private sector.[33] In many cases where the individual lives some distance from VA facilities, continuous hospitalization is necessary if treatment is to be offered to the veteran.

Third, and probably most significant, is the fact that VA treatment is "free" and patients tend to overstay in hospitals. Persons treated in the VA system have no economic incentive to curtail length of stay other than time lost on a job, and hospital administrators appear lenient in allowing patients to remain in hospitals who might be cared for at home. Since the VA serves a large medically indigent clientele it may be guessed that hospital stays may serve as a respite from outside conditions. Free care and attention is a pleasant luxury to many indigent veterans, and it is unlikely that they are always eager to leave.

The comparative data on duration of stay in VA and community hospitals have their limitation for purposes of analyzing VA operations or applying the implications to a broader national health delivery system. The overutilization of VA hospital facilities must be considered in light of the historical factors that might account for longer average stays than experienced in community hospitals. As a system whose original justification was solely to care for the war damaged, it was natural that the VA limited its coverage to hospital care. But over the years the VA health role has expanded, and its hospitals have tried to fill a number of functions which community hospitals have never accepted, but delegated instead to other institutions and private homes. For many years VA hospitals have officially and unofficially provided nursing care to the indigent, a role which no cost-conscious hospital could afford. And in the absence of adequate facilities many VA hospitals still are forced to perform other functions of nursing care or to provide hotel facilities for patients who cannot commute for needed posthospital care. At the same time, the VA's one-stop, cure-everything approach provided outpatient services on an in-house basis. These factors, plus the obvious lack of financial incentive to cut down on hospital use, have resulted in substantial "overuse."

The argument that free care tempts indigents to overstay their illnesses implies that the decision to remain in the hospital is made solely by patients. Especially in VA hospitals, it is the doctor who has the most responsibility for patient tenure. Doctors have no financial incentive either to shorten or lengthen patients' stays, and it is specious to argue that doctors conspire to waste money by keeping patients unduly long. Undoubtedly the lack of cost pressure on either doctor or patient does not tend to minimize patient stays. But that the patients are receiving superfluous care is not so clear. The community hospital alternative, in which doctor and patient alike race against their pocketbooks to get the patient propped on his feet and out of his hospital bed is surely not an ideal solution.

By relieving hospitals of their lingering roles as nursing homes and one-stop medical shops, and by actively urging doctors to terminate unnecessary hospitalization, the VA could certainly cut its average hospital stays significantly. Given the nature of the clientele and thoroughness of the care delivered, however, it would be unrealistic and probably undesirable to expect VA hospitals to match community hospitals' average patient stay. But if a significantly reduced average stay could be added to the VA's already low cost per diem delivery of health care, the system could become a model for public health care.

The VA and National Health Care

The burdens of bearing the cost of medical care are steadily being shifted to the federal government. In line with these developments, Congress recently proposed that VA medical care should be extended to cover outpatient services for nonservice-connected cases.[34] Except for immediate care provided to emergency cases, regulations rule out the use of outpatient clinics to provide preventative care to a large sector of prospective hospital clientele. Advocates of expanding VA preventative care argue that since the costs of care for nonservice-connected cases will eventually fall upon the taxpayer through the VA, Medicare, or Medicaid, preventative care appears most practical. It would reduce costs and conserve medical resources, and better serve clients by providing care in the early stages of the ailment. A 1972 bill which President Nixon vetoed would have broadened access to outpatient services to include care which "is reasonably necessary to obviate the need for hospital admission." The same argument might be made in favor of national health insurance for all Americans, and not just veterans.

The steady expansion of VA medical responsibility has resulted in a national hospital system which apparently can be organized and run to deliver above-average care to high numbers at a reasonable cost. The shortcomings of the VA system, notably its built-in overstay, point up the problems of delivering "free" health care. Obviously an efficient health care system must insure that only those who actually need hospitalization receive it, while those who need nursing, ambulatory, psychiatric, or domiciliary care are directed to these services. The VA's one-stop system has tended to make hospitals responsible for all these kinds of care, even when the services were available elsewhere. But this example of the VA's weaknesses should be valuable to planners of the government's future role in the delivery of health care. The VA experience demonstrates that government-run medical care can be efficient, and suggests that free medical care could be successfully delivered to those who need it most. Compared with the brief history of Medicaid administration, the VA example is encouraging.

It should be recognized that as the right to good health is extended to all through nationally subsidized health programs, the justification for a separate VA system will become much weaker. Over the years spokesmen for the VA have insisted that care for those wounded in battle can best be delivered along with a variety of other types of care, and the VA has practiced what its spokesmen advocated. Based on this experience there is no reason to fear that the government's responsibility to its war damaged will be compromised by melding it with the government's developing responsibility to keep all its people healthy. A single national health care system would be to the advantage of all and the VA system may be an excellent model from which to plan for this system.

CHAPTER 4

Back to Civilian Life

They shall beat their swords into plowshares,
and their spears into pruning-hooks.

Isaiah 2:4

The Problems They Face

Over 6 million veterans were separated from military service during the first eight years of the Vietnam era, starting on August 4, 1964.
Almost two million of these veterans drifted back into civilian life in
fiscal years 1970 and 1971, and an additional three-quarters of a million
more during the succeeding year. Less than two percent of these veterans were women.

Approximately 40 percent have seen duty in Vietnam. Medical
and other technological advances have kept alive many injured servicemen who would have perished in previous wars, leaving 308,800 veterans with service-connected disabilities by mid-1972. These included
7.4 percent totally disabled, most of them permanently.

All of these veterans are subject to the usual aspirations, anxieties,
and needs of young adults, but many also have particular problems
resulting from their recent military service and their reentry into
civilian life. Though many have not experienced difficulty in making
the transition to work, education, or some other endeavor, other veterans have faced adjustment problems that are frequently directly or
indirectly related to their stint of service.

These veterans have reentered civilian society after an average of
2.8 years in the military. Many came directly from combat areas. All
have undergone an interruption in their normal lives, leaving jobs or
schools to enter military service. For some, the opportunity to work or
to continue school was disrupted even before entry into the armed
forces, because they knew that military service was inevitable.

Upon returning, the veteran frequently bore the brunt of societal
ambivalence toward the war and toward the men who fought in Vietnam. In a special report on the employment problems of the Vietnam
veterans, the National Advisory Council on Vocational Education ex-
pressed the country's mood:

Once again the veterans return from war. The situation is not novel
in our history, yet somehow these veterans seem different. They do

105

not return to triumphant parades as in the past, nor do they want them. . . . They do not fit the image of returning heroes. . . .

The unpopularity of the war places an additional burden upon the returning veteran. The young veteran finds himself referred to in print and in conversation as a dope addict or trained killer. Often his own peer group tells him what a fool he was to go to Vietnam in the first place. In his absence they have moved ahead in their life pursuits . . . while the veteran . . . must start from the beginning as though his military service made no difference.[1]

The increasing opposition to the Vietnam war created a less than supportive atmosphere for some veterans. In many cases these young men have returned isolated from, and to some degree alienated from, their peer groups and society at large. As a result, they have had to make psychological and social adjustments in addition to the other adjustments they had to face in civilian life.

Drug addiction has been a major problem, though it is not exclusively a veteran phenomenon. In addition, there were other health problems, minor and major, physical and mental, attributable to service hardships and conditions, for which the veteran needed treatment.

Another critical problem for many veterans was employment (chart 17). The decline in the Vietnam commitment and accompanying reduction in the size of the armed forces coincided with an economic recession. At a time when the Vietnam era veteran returned to society in the greatest numbers, the nation witnessed its highest unemployment rates in recent years. It was not until 1972, when the economy began to recover, that the unemployment situation for veterans began to improve. The added dimension of the often unsuccessful job hunt became another burden for the veteran to bear. Because more veterans than nonveterans are reentrants or new entrants into the labor market, higher rates of unemployment are not an unexpected problem. However, the availability of readjustment benefits may modify the veterans' reentry into the labor market. Help is available from many public and private sources to assist the veteran in conducting his job search, returning to school or training, or collecting unemployment compensation benefits. Educational benefits may delay a recently separated veteran's reentry into the labor market and the availability of unemployment compensation may affect his selection of a job. Nonveterans looking for work may not have such a wide range of choices.

The Vietnam Veteran

More than three of every four Vietnam veterans in 1972 were still in their twenties. While the average age of the total Vietnam veteran population was 27.6 years, the average age of separatees between 1965

CHART 17

UNEMPLOYMENT RATES OF VETERANS AND NONVETERANS, 1969–1972

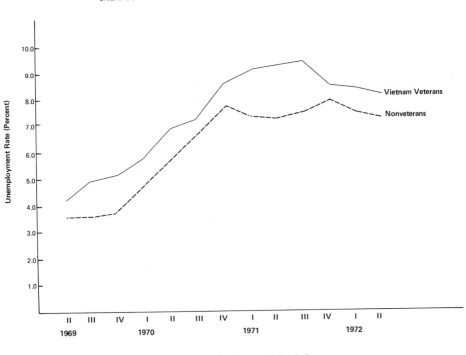

Source: U.S. Department of Labor, Bureau of Labor Statistics, *Employment and Earnings,* April
1972, Table 21, p.137, and July 1972, Table 21, p. 134.
Note: Seasonally adjusted data for 20 to 29 year-old men only.

and 1972 was 23.[2] Because they were young, the veterans shared the
problems that plagued all youth in our nation—those of defining
ideals and goals; of assuming responsibilities; and, more importantly,
for their purposes, of obtaining further education and/or training
while facing extremely high levels of unemployment.

The veterans' education and/or training may have been either
directly or indirectly curbed because of military service. However, the
young veteran was better educated than his predecessors of World War
II or Korea. Fewer Vietnam veterans failed to finish their elementary
education and more went on to complete high school. Only 45 percent
of World War II veterans had attained at least a high school education
upon leaving the military, compared to 80 percent of Vietnam veterans. The Vietnam veteran had no more college education, however,
than his counterparts in earlier wars. In fact, he was slightly less likely
to have earned a college diploma because he was younger at the time
of his entrance into the military.

The educational attainment of Vietnam veterans also varied

significantly from the nonveterans in the same age group (chart 18).
Relatively few veterans had gone to college compared with their nonveteran counterparts. However, more had completed high school than
nonveterans. Two major reasons account for the differences in educational level of veterans and others in the same age bracket. First,
youths who entered college obtained deferments for continued education and those who failed to finish high school—concentrated heavily
among the poor—were most likely to fail either the mental or physical
tests for entry into military service. Thus, the veterans were underrepresented in both the higher and lower educational levels. Another

CHART 18
EDUCATIONAL ATTAINMENT OF VIETNAM VETERANS AND
NONVETERANS AGED 20 TO 29 IN 1971

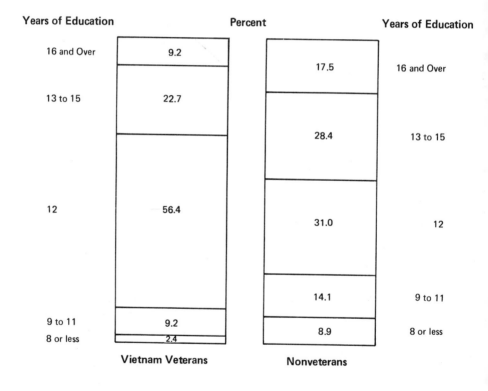

Years of Education	Percent		Years of Education
16 and Over	9.2	17.5	16 and Over
13 to 15	22.7	28.4	13 to 15
12	56.4	31.0	12
		14.1	9 to 11
9 to 11	9.2	8.9	8 or less
8 or less	2.4		

Vietnam Veterans   Nonveterans

Source: Elizabeth Waldman and Kathryn R. Gover, "Employment Situation of Vietnam Era
Veterans, " *Monthly Labor Review*, September 1971, p. 10.

factor which contributed to the high percentage of high school graduates among veterans was the opportunity to complete high school
equivalency courses while in the service.

Many veterans probably postponed marriage until they finished
military service. Thirty-one percent of enlisted personnel separating
from the military during 1970 were married soldiers, compared with
more than half of all the young Vietnam veterans (20 to 24 years old)
in civilian life.[3] The resulting family responsibilities augmented the
veteran's readjustment difficulties. Certainly, this affected his decisions
as he examined his priorities and the opportunities available to him.

The racial composition of Vietnam veterans was slightly different
than that of civilians who did not serve. There was a smaller proportion of minority veterans than minority nonveterans among men 20 to
29 years of age—9.1 and 12.9 percent, respectively. This is largely
attributable to two factors: higher reenlistment rates for black servicemen and a higher percentage of blacks failing to meet the physical and
mental requirements to enter the military. Minority veterans were
subject to additional social and economic disadvantages that accentu-
ated their transitional problems (chart 19).

Work and Training Experience

The average age of the veteran separatees, 23, was an age when
many of the veterans would have and many of their nonveteran peers
had in fact finished college and begun their first job. Others among
the nonveterans had completed some post-high school training and
progressed in a skilled occupation for a year or more. Still others had
been employed throughout the period and had gained valuable work
experience, beginning to move up the occupational or income ladder.
This was not true for the returning Vietnam veteran.

Due to his youth, the Vietnam veteran had little preservice work
experience. Although information about this experience is limited,
former Assistant Secretary of Labor Malcolm Lovell, in testimony before the Senate Committee on Labor and Public Welfare, estimated
that at least 350,000, or one-third of the 1970 separatees from military
service were employed before entering military service.[4] Whatever the
exact figures, any preservice work experience they may have had was
probably in either unskilled or semiskilled occupations, due to the
youth and relative lack of education of most men entering service.

Veterans with little valuable preservice work experience and
limited formal education were not generally offered salable skills or
education while in the military. A survey by Louis Harris in August
1971 found that 44 percent of returning veterans stated that they received no occupational training while in the military. Of those who

CHART 19

MINORITY VETERANS FACED UNEMPLOYMENT RATES MORE THAN 50 PERCENT
GREATER THAN WHITE VETERANS

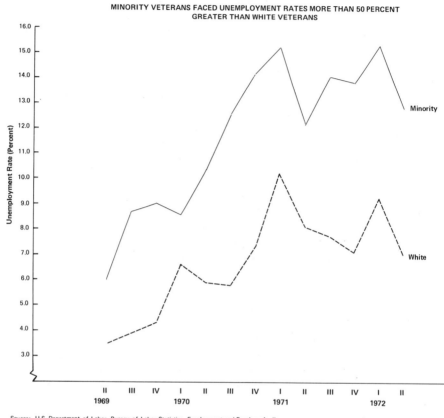

Source: U.S. Department of Labor, Bureau of Labor Statistics, *Employment and Earnings,*, April
          1972, Table 20. p. 134, and July 1972, Table 20, p. 131.

Note: Seasonally unadjusted data for 20 to 29 year old men only.

served between 6 months and 2 years, this figure rose to 58 percent. Moreover, there is a definite relationship between the branch of service and occupational training received. Seven of every ten Navy and Air Force veterans responded that they had acquired skill training, while less than half of Army and Marine veterans felt they had been taught a skill.[5]

While acquiring a skill in the military was difficult, transferring that skill to a civilian job was more frustrating for the veteran. A Louis Harris survey found that over half the veterans who received occupational training felt that the training was only slightly useful or not useful at all. Employers who hired veterans rated military experience somewhat higher. Three of five employers surveyed felt military experience was helpful to the veteran.

Another study found that technical skills acquired in the Air

Force were transferable to civilian life. Veterans who attained such skills enjoyed higher incomes, greater job satisfaction, and consequently retained positive reactions to military training.[6] But a similar investigation of Army and Navy training disclosed that military experience did little to raise the future income of veterans, especially those assigned to combat and other nontechnical specialties. The Vietnam veterans who were in combat-related military occupations or in service and supply handling, for example, received little or no skill training transferable to civilian life. Often veterans assigned during their military career to jobs requiring technical or craft tasks found that training was either inadequate or too specialized to be adaptable to civilian occupations. Other veterans either could not or did not desire to enter occupational fields for which they were trained in the military.[7]

However, closer examination of the postservice experience of veterans reveal other factors more significant to the veteran's success. Robert Richardson found that formal education was clearly a significant element in the transferability process.[8] Since the military generally selects servicemen for training according to mental aptitude tests and previous education, the problem is compounded. Those with the greatest need for skill training were the least often selected for this training and more often ended up in military occupations which are least transferable to civilian occupations. Weinstein, too, found that among Army and Navy veterans, preservice education and experience was important. Men who previously held civilian jobs related to their military occupational specialty were more successful in transferring their skills back to civilian jobs. For other men, preservice education was an important determinant of postmilitary success in the labor market.[9]

Over one-third of the men separated from the service during 1970 were in combat-related or service occupational specialties (chart 20). For blacks, the proportion was one-half. These men were unable to transfer their military experience to civilian jobs. Their preservice experience was most likely limited. The readjustment benefits offered to veterans are of added importance to these men as they reenter civilian life.

Despite the problems veterans experience in readjusting to the civilian labor market, after they are reabsorbed their earnings exceeded those of their nonveteran counterparts (table 22). In 1970, young veterans (20–24 years old) employed full time earned over $800 more than young nonveterans. The earnings differential of older (25–29 years old) veterans and nonveterans who worked full time was less than $100 annually. Veterans who did not work during the year had incomes about six times greater than comparable nonveterans. This was because the veterans' reported income was inflated with military pay and veterans' benefits.

CHART 20

ONE–HALF OF THE BLACKS AND ONE–THIRD OF THE WHITES SEPARATING
FROM THE ARMED SERVICES IN 1970 WERE IN MILITARY OCCUPATIONS NOT
READILY TRANSFERABLE TO CIVILIAN LIFE

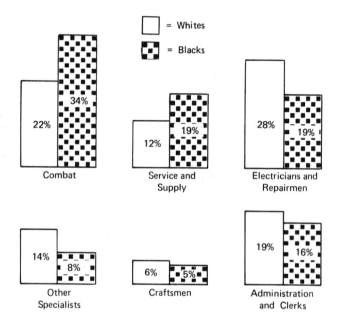

Source: Eli S. Flyer, "Profile of DOD First-Term Enlisted Personnel Separating from
Active Service During 1970," *Manpower Research Note*, Office of the Assistant
Secretary of Defense, October 1971, Table II.

The "typical" Vietnam veteran in 1972 was a 27 year old high
school graduate. When he left the military he was 23 years old. He
reentered society much as he left it, except that he was a few years
older and had missed whatever opportunities were available to those
who were left behind. But many had encountered obstacles that hin-
dered their readjustment. Some were disabled and many had other
health problems; some were drug addicts; some were alienated, and
many were unemployed. And like other young blacks, Chicanos, and
American Indians, minority veterans found that discrimination continued to be a barrier to opportunities in civilian life.

Table 22. In 1970 Veterans Had Higher Incomes than Nonveterans
with Similar Work Experience

Work Experience	Veterans		Nonveterans	
	Percent	Median Personal Income	Percent	Median Personal Income
Men, 20 to 24 years old	100	$4,438	100	$3,334
Full time	41	7,270	42	6,402
Part time	43	3,747	48	2,087
Did not work	16	2,741	9	less than $500
Men, 25 to 29 years old	100	$7,634	100	$7,625
Full time	67	8,635	72	8,525
Part time	29	5,350	24	5,188
Did not work	4	3,353	4	less than $500

Source: Elizabeth Waldman and Kathryn R. Gover, "Employment Situation of Vietnam Era Veterans," Monthly Labor Review, September 1971, p. 8.

The Readjustment Kit

Upon their return to civilian life, veterans must compete with their peers who have had opportunities to progress in their education, training, or work. Some veterans may have already finished their formal education before entering the service or in military classrooms. Others may need further education or training to advance in their career plan. Although the process of informing servicemen of their postservice options for employment and education begins while they are still in the military, some may need encouragement and direction when they return to civilian life. Counseling, then, is the first step in the veteran's readjustment. An evaluation of the individual's goals and needs with the help of a counselor leads the veteran into choosing among the direct routes to jobs and the various education and training programs in which he can enroll. The veteran's options are not dissimilar from his nonveteran peers. However, the readjustment benefits available for veterans may influence his decisions.

The forms of assistance offered to the veteran were varied. Some servicemen were offered counseling and training before discharge. The law required employers to place the newly-discharged veteran in his preservice job. Moreover, federal and most state and local governments offered preference to veterans applying for jobs. For the veteran who could not find a job, the government provided a cushion in the form of unemployment benefits. Finally, the government offered assistance to veterans who opted for added education and training. Disabled veterans received special consideration in most readjustment programs.

Approximately $2.5 billion was spent during fiscal 1972 on education and vocational rehabilitation, unemployment compensation, and housing loans for veterans. Several hundred million more dollars were expended for public employment, manpower training, and employment assistance for veterans who received preference in programs generally available to the public. No precise estimate of the latter expenditures is available, however, since such programs do not earmark funds for veterans.

Project Transition

Readjustment assistance to the prospective veteran starts in the armed forces. Since 1967 the military has operated a modest program to counsel and train servicemen prior to their return to civilian life. The program, dubbed Project Transition, focused initially on the vocational training needs of unskilled and deficiently educated military personnel. Since then, Project Transition has expanded to include counseling to help all those who want assistance in finding a civilian job. Moreover, the President's veterans' program, announced in June 1971, urged that the military not only expand the stateside programs, but also find more ways to provide services to those stationed in Europe and Asia.

The vocational training offered under Project Transition is sponsored by private industry, by the Department of Labor's Manpower Development and Training Act (MDTA) funds, and by other government agencies including the military. Armed forces educational programs are not formally part of Project Transition, but remain options to which some men may be referred. Formal industry training covers a variety of automotive and repair occupations as well as sales and computer-related jobs. MDTA training includes many of the same occupations, but also provides courses offered by the building trades unions and the International Association of Chiefs of Police. MDTA national contracts require that some job placement assistance be given to the men who take these courses. The United States Armed Forces Institute (USAFI) offers some vocational training through correspondence courses and contracts with schools to offer vocational and technical courses to servicemen. Some 200,000 servicemen received training under Project Transition in its first five years, including 65,000 in fiscal 1972. They were trained at over 200 military installations in the United States.

The costs of Project Transition training are generally borne by the sponsors of the classes, not by the military itself. Forty percent of the training is offered by private industry. Another forty percent is financed by Labor Department funds at an estimated cost of $10 million in fiscal year 1972.[10] The Department of Defense bears only a small portion of the direct costs of Project Transition training in military classrooms, although incurring the indirect costs of releasing men from active duty and allowing the use of military facilities for some programs. Most of the Defense Department's Project Transition budget of $16 million in 1972 was spent on counseling activities.

Men with less than a high school education are encouraged to take the USAFI General Education Development (GED) tests to obtain a certificate for an eighth grade education or a high school diploma. The Defense Department estimates that 82,000 men successfully completed the high school GED examination during fiscal year 1972. In addition, the 1970 amendments to the GI bill provided for a Predischarge Education Program (PREP) for deficiently educated servicemen with at least 180 days of active duty. PREP programs are conducted by colleges with Veterans Administration funds and in cooperation with the military. These courses concentrate on improving the basic reading and mathematics skills to bring disadvantaged servicemen up to the level of high school graduates. The 1972 Vietnam Era Veterans Readjustment Assistance Act urged the military and the VA to expand PREP courses, particularly overseas, and mandated changes to make it easier for servicemen to take the courses. For example, the minimum class time was reduced from 25 to 12 hours per week, half of which time could be taken from active duty.

Although skill training was originally the major goal of Project Transition, perhaps its most significant contribution to veterans' readjustment has become the counseling programs; the intent is to stimulate interest among the soldiers to avail themselves of opportunities for education and employment assistance after discharge. The skill training and career planning needed by young servicemen require more time, resources, and individual attention than the military is able to provide.

The Project Transition program has been plagued by several inherent problems as well as a few unforeseen difficulties. First, the size and worldwide distribution of military installations means that although counseling is available at each base, training opportunities vary. Many men may take whatever course is offered, whether or not they intend to use the training in civilian life. Also, lack of command support despite directives from the Pentagon is apparently a barrier to successful programs at some bases.

Because skill training in the combat areas of Vietnam was obviously impractical, the military established skill training centers in the United States for men returning from combat duty. By the end of 1972, over 9,000 men had been trained at the 23 skill centers established on military bases.

The nature of the training itself may also cause problems. While they are still carrying military responsibilities, most enrollees receive only part-time training for a total of 240 hours. Although in some courses, such as police training and automotive skills sponsored by Ford and General Motors, the 240 hours is an acceptable credential, it is doubtful whether such limited formal training is readily accepable to civilian employers. A vocational program in drafting or electronics at a civilian institute, for example, consists of over 2,000 hours of training.[11] MDTA-Institutional courses usually consist of five or six months (or over 800 hours) of classwork. Because little follow-up information has been collected, neither the military nor the Department of Labor is certain about the success of the Project Transition program.

Developing job opportunities for men in the vocational programs is also quite difficult when so many men leave the area after training. National contractors, like the United Brotherhood of Carpenters and Joiners; government agencies, like the Postal Service; and major private companies gain one possible advantage, however, from the geographic mobility of the men. They are able to train a variety of men at a central location without having to absorb all the graduates into a single labor market.

The economic recession and the military's early release policy are among the unpredictable problems which affected Project Transition. The recession economy may possibly have affected the transition program more than other training programs since private companies could get all the help they needed in a slack labor market without investing their own resources in the training of potential workers. The difficulties of the program were compounded by the reduction in military forces in 1971 and 1972 resulting in early release of many servicemen. Men returning from Vietnam were generally discharged immediately upon their return to the United States and therefore did not benefit from vocational training under Project Transition.

Reaching Out to Veterans

Once the serviceman leaves the armed forces, the major governmental responsibility for his readjustment to civilian life rests with the Veterans Administration. Traditionally the VA has had an open door policy and largely limited its services to veterans who came knocking at the agency's doors. The veteran, either by himself or through the auspices of one of the service veterans' organizations, found his way to the VA offices. This situation was particularly true for the nondisabled veteran who might seek education or training benefits. After the Veterans Readjustment Act of 1966 was passed, however, Vietnam veterans did not make use of the benefits to the extent anticipated, based on the experience of earlier programs. To overcome the reluctance of Vietnam veterans to apply for readjustment benefits, the VA initiated Operation Outreach in 1968. This effort extended the responsibilities of the contact division of the VA, which is reponsible for the first contact with the veteran. Major efforts have been made to increase the veteran's awareness of benefits and to induce him to apply for VA assistance. VA counseling, budgeted at $7.5 million during 1972, depends heavily on education and training benefits as a source of readjustment for the veteran.[12]

The Department of Defense cooperated with the Veterans Administration's outreach efforts by the dissemination of information in Vietnam combat zones. Experienced VA contact men were assigned to different locations in Vietnam and other areas where troops were stationed. Group orientation was normally the procedure followed, but individual assistance was also available to veterans who desired it. Another form of outreach was a bedside assistance program which attempted to inform servicemen or veterans in hospitals about their benefits and to aid them in initial applications. The VA stationed its contact representatives in over 180 military hospitals as well as all veteran's hospitals. The VA has also made contact personnel and counselors available at various separation centers for servicemen in the United States. These services were provided at over 300 separation points, from an "on call" basis in some places to a seven days a week operation at some of the large West Coast centers processing servicemen returning from Vietnam.

The Department of Defense supplied the VA with a copy of the release papers of each person leaving the service, including educational and other relevant information. A special letter, tailored to the educational circumstances of the veteran, was then sent to each veteran. The letter informed the veteran of the educational and training benefits available, pointed out those most suitable for him, and encouraged him to call and speak personally with a VA representative. Six months later a second letter was mailed. The VA went to considerable lengths to make the response as painless as possible by installing a toll-free telephone system in 59 larger cities and in six states. If the veteran did not respond to the first letter, two additional follow-up efforts were made over a period of several months. The veteran was dropped from the list of those being actively solicited after no response had been made to these three letters plus possible attempts at telephone contact. The VA officials consider their outreach efforts extremely successful. Over a third of the veterans receiving letters responded and 47 percent of these requested a return telephone call for further assistance.[13]

Another recent addition to the arsenal of services and facilities available to the veteran are the United States Veterans Assistance Centers (USVACs), established to smooth the delivery of services to the recently separated veteran by bringing together a range of services he might need into a one-stop center. The need for a one-stop center was particularly evident in the major urban areas with heavy concentrations of veterans. A network of 72 centers has been established since 1968, mostly as part of the 57 VA regional offices. Representatives from various other agencies were also located in the centers to augment the services provided by the VA. Some areas, such as Los Angeles and Washington, D.C., had separate centers located in areas where minority groups are heavily concentrated.

The United States Civil Service Commission and the United States Employment Service were represented in the centers and contact was maintained with community action groups, housing authorities, the National Urban League, and others. Social workers were added to the staffs in 1969 to offer further assistance to the veteran. Special efforts were made by center personnel to help veterans without a high school education.

The VA may well have the most extensive operation to reach its potential clientele of any government agency. Not only did the agency have a captive audience in the initial outreach activities at the separation points and the hospitals, but it also persisted in reaching veterans in their home. For example, in Texas the VA sent mobile vans staffed with counselors, a social worker, and a state employment interviewer to the rural areas in an attempt to reach disadvantaged veterans who had never seen the inside of a VA office. Other government agencies complemented the VA efforts. To help bring VA services to low income veterans, the Office of Economic Opportunity funded outreach operations in a dozen cities. The Appalachian Regional Commission and the Urban Coalition were also involved. The veterans apparently welcomed this attention. According to a Louis Harris survey, over 60 percent of the veterans interviewed said they appreciated being contacted and two-thirds of the men felt that the VA could be visited conveniently.[14]

Although it is impossible to determine the extent of the veterans' awareness or knowledge of their benefits or the impact of the outreach program in broadening their information, the effect appears significant. Certainly the attempts have been and continue to be prodigious and the contacts frequent. Whatever the reasons, the participation in the programs has been increasing quite rapidly, particularly in the education and training program. There are continuing efforts to inform those who have not chosen to use their benefits of their alternatives, to encourage them to participate, and to overcome any other impediments that deter the veterans from readjusting successfully.

Unemployment Compensation

In addition to the various services, income support has been an integral part of the veterans' readjustment kit since World War II. Upon leaving the military, veterans of World War II and Korea were given a "mustering-out pay" of $300 if they had served over sixty days and spent some part of their duty outside the United States. Those who only served inside the country were given $200 and those who spent less than sixty days in the armed forces were given $100. This severance pay was available to all enlisted men and officers below the rank of major or lieutenant commander. As of July 1, 1966, mustering-out pay was repealed by Congress. Thus, most Vietnam veterans can only collect their accrued leave payment, although six states provide "bonus payments" of $100 to $300 to their residents upon return from duty.

Unemployment compensation for veterans was first included in the Veterans Readjustment Act of 1944. Out of the 16.1 million World War II veterans, 59 percent collected unemployment benefits and joined the "52–20 Club," based on the provision of the law which allowed for a maximum of 52 weeks of compensation at $20 per week. The income support served as a cushion to a majority of veterans. A total of $4 billion was spent by the federal government between the signing of the bill on June 22, 1944 and July 25, 1949, when the program ended.

The 1952 Korean GI bill (Veterans Readjustment Assistance Act of 1952) and later amendments again provided for unemployment benefits for those men who served after June 26, 1950. The maximum length of benefits was reduced to 26 weeks and the amount that could be collected was raised to $26 per week. Responsibility for administration of the program was delegated to the state unemployment insurance agencies. During the nine and a half year period that the law remained in effect, 1.3 million Korean veterans, or 19 percent of those who served during the war, collected $454 million in benefits.

The Ex-Servicemen's Compensation Act of 1958 established a permanent system of unemployment insurance, and included peacetime veterans for the first time. Veterans are eligible for unemployment compensation payments (UCX) within one year after they are honorably discharged following at least 90 days of active military service. The time requirement can be waived for those discharged due to a service-connected disability. Until 1970 veterans were ineligible to collect unemployment benefits until their accrued leave had expired. While they can register in most states immediately upon their release from active duty, some states postpone benefits for the duration of the accrued leave.

In establishing his claim, the veteran is subject to the laws of the state in which he files. For the most part, a veteran can choose the state in which he wants to file as long as he has an address established there. After initiating his claim, he can move to another state and collect his benefits under the interstate claims system. He thus has an advantage in being able to choose a state where he will collect a higher payment. Maximum payments for unemployment insurance (excluding dependents' allowances) varied in 1972 from $45 a week in Indiana to $105 a week in the District of Columbia.

Unemployment insurance claimants must be available for full time employment and must actively seek work. In some states, however, veterans enrolled in school or training under the GI bill may receive both their UCX payment and GI bill stipend. In other states, unemployment payments to GI bill recipients are reduced. Still other state laws prohibit the collection of both.

Just as eligibility is determined by state law, so is the amount of the payment that the veteran receives. This level of payments is based upon the previous earnings of the unemployed worker. Because military cash payments are relatively low compared with civilian wages, federal law establishes presumed comparability to compensate for military in-kind compensation. This schedule yielded average weekly benefits of $56 per week in fiscal 1972, almost equal to those paid to nonveterans.

In most states, the maximum duration of benefits is 26 weeks in any 52-week period, and federal law provides for extended benefits in states with high unemployment. But most veterans leave the unemployment rolls before they exhaust benefits. In 1972, veterans qualifying for unemployment benefits remained on the rolls for 14.5 weeks, compared with the average claim of 14.4 weeks by nonveterans. The VA offers special help to those unemployed for long periods. After 12 weeks, the state unemployment insurance office notifies the VA of the veteran's status and the agency again attempts to reach him to advise him of the assistance available to find him a job or an education or training program.

The total amount of benefits paid increased more than tenfold between 1967 and 1972 (chart 21). Not only has the average duration of veterans' claims and the average weekly payment increased, but the

CHART 21

APPROXIMATELY $1 BILLION HAS BEEN PAID IN UNEMPLOYMENT COMPENSATION TO EX–SERVICEMEN IN THE PAST SIX YEARS

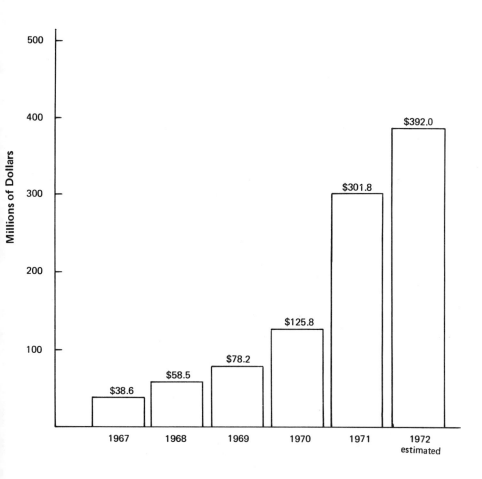

Source: U.S. Department of Labor, Unemployment Insurance Service, unpublished tables.

number of veterans establishing claims and collecting benefits had increased steadily. Two major factors accounted for the increase. First, as a result of improved counseling, more Vietnam veterans have been made aware of the availability of unemployment compensation. And, more important, unemployment benefits served as a buffer in a period when jobs were scarce in the recession.

Helping Veterans Find a Job

The veteran's readjustment began with counseling in the military or from the VA on what forms of employment or education were open to him. If he had difficulty in finding employment, he could collect unemployment compensation to cushion his return to civilian life. The Louis Harris survey found that 55 percent of all Vietnam veterans collected unemployment benefits.[15] To help the veteran find employment, the law provides him several direct routes to employment—reemployment rights in his preservice job, preference in civil service appointments, and special consideration under the United States Employment Service.

Reemployment Rights

To provide for men who left jobs to enter the military, reemployment rights for veterans have existed since 1940. Men and women who leave permanent jobs may claim reemployment in their old jobs. In the case of disabled veterans, the Department of Labor's Office of Reemployment Rights attempts to place the incapacitated veteran in a position whose duties he can perform. Employers are required to retain a veteran for at least one year unless he is discharged or laid off for proper cause.[16]

Veterans must generally apply for reemployment within 90 days of their discharge, although special extensions are available for the disabled. Altogether only 6,900 veterans contacted the Labor Department in 1971 for reemployment assistance. This represents less than one percent of all those who separated from the military during the year and only about one of every 50 of these cases was referred to the Justice Department for litigation. Most employers apparently cooperated with the law and relatively few cases required public attention.

Preference in Civil Service Employment

Although veterans' preference was traditional in federal government hiring practices before the end of World War II, the Veterans' Preference Act of 1944 clearly defined the civil service regulations for hiring veterans. Disabled veterans are eligible for an additional 10 points and other veterans for an extra 5 points on their civil service examination sources. If a veteran is disabled to the extent that he could not take a civil service appointment, his wife is eligible for his veterans' preference rights. A widow of a serviceman is also able to claim her husband's preference if she should choose to enter federal employment. Other aspects of the law provide those claiming veterans' preference with priority in reemployment and reinstatement in the federal civil service. And should a reduction in force occur, they have preference in retaining their jobs.

Recent additions to veterans' preference regulations for Vietnam veterans have made it easier for them to enter the federal civil service and to upgrade themselves. Since April 1970 federal agencies have been able to offer veterans noncompetitive appointments in jobs with an annual pay of $7,694 or less (grades 1 through 5, 1973 pay scales). These appointments are convertible to career positions provided the veteran completes a self-development program.[17] Appointments to jobs paying less than $6,128 (grade level 3 and below) can be made on the basis of the veteran's military experience provided that the agency feels he can perform the duties of the job.

Of greater significance is the preference accorded veterans in state and local jobs, though practices vary widely. While federal employment remained relatively stable in recent years, state and local payrolls continued to expand even during the 1970 recession when aggregate private employment stagnated and even declined. In the first eight years of the Vietnam era, state and local employment rose by more than 3 million jobs. Vietnam veterans took advantage of the employment opportunities offered to them in public service and black veterans have used these opportunities to a greater extent than whites. During mid-1971, 24 percent of employed black Vietnam veterans were in government jobs, compared with 12 percent of whites:[18]

	White	Black
Percent distribution	100	100
Private wage and salary	85	74
Government	12	24
Self-employed and unpaid	4	2

Their Job Search

Placement services of the more than 2,000 local offices of the United States Employment Service (USES) are available to all unemployed persons in search of jobs. Veterans have been singled out for special services since the USES was established under the Wagner-Peyser Act in 1933. While other special groups have been spotlighted over the years for the attention of the USES, priority for veterans has been maintained.[19]

The majority of Vietnam veterans who have claimed unemployment benefits are also exposed to the public employment service, since most state laws require that persons collecting unemployment compensation benefits sign up for work at the employment service. But exposure to a local employment service may not help a veteran to find employment if employers fail to register their job vacancies or if the labor market information available is incomplete.

To augment the number of openings, Executive Order 11598 (June 18, 1971) required federal agencies and government contractors and subcontractors to list most job vacancies paying less than $18,000 annually with the local offices of the employment service. Veterans were to receive preference in referral to the jobs.[20] It was hoped that 1.2 million such listings would be made available during the 1972 fiscal year. But hampered by a slow start and surrounded by confusion as to what was actually required of the government contractors, at the outset few jobs were registered as a result of the "mandatory listings" and few Vietnam veterans benefited initially by the new policy. Aside from the payment of unemployment benefits, the assistance offered by public employment offices to veterans remained marginal. During 1972, however, the employment service reported an increase in the number of nonagricultural jobs listed in its local offices for the first time in five years. And the number of placements of Vietnam veterans rose substantially over the previous years' performance. What portion of these improvements were due to the executive order or the re-vitalized veterans' preference policies is uncertain.

Education and Training

Returning to an interrupted education or embarking on a new program for education or training is not easy for a 23 year old vet-eran. Scholarship funds were often not as accessible to him as to the 18 year old high school graduate. Lack of money or poor performance at school or a job may have been one of the major factors contributing to the initial drafting or enlistment of the veteran into the service. Even when funds were available to him, he had to compete with other veterans and nonveterans for woefully inadequate scholarship funds or loans. Parental financial aid, possibly available at 18, may not have been forthcoming for the older veteran, or may not be accepted. Although other problems contributed to choices other than the return to school, inadequate finances was a major factor which limited further education and training. Most did not need special services or other intensive or extensive efforts on their behalf—what they needed was money.

Financial assistance for education and training of veterans return-ing to civilian society has historically been provided by the various "GI bills." Education and training assistance constitutes the largest single readjustment benefit for veterans both in amount of money spent and in number of veterans using it. During the 26 years follow-

Table 23. The Three GI Bills Have Provided Education Benefits to 13.5 Million Veterans at a Cost of $24.6 Billion

	Total	World War II	Korean Conflict	Post-Korea (to June 1972)
Eligible (millions)	30.4	15.6	5.7	9.1
Trained (millions)	13.5	7.8	2.4	3.3
Cost (billions)	$24.6	$14.5	$4.5	$5.6

Source: U.S. Veterans Administration, *Veterans Benefits Under Current Educational Programs*, Department of Veterans Benefits Information Bulletin 24–72–6, June 1972, p. 30; and "Veterans' Affairs," *Congress and the Nation, 1965–1968* (Washington: Congressional Quarterly, 1969), p. 456.

ing World War II, some 13.5 million veterans have participated in education and training programs at a cost of over $24.6 billion (table 23).

The Vietnam Program

As of June 1972, some 3.1 million veterans had received education and training assistance under the 1966 GI bill at a cost of $5.6 billion. Seven of ten were Vietnam era veterans. Another 267,000 servicemen received education or training assistance while in the military service. More veterans turned to education and training during the early seventies than in the preceeding years. This occurred not only because the total number of veterans increased, but also because job opportunities were scarce during the recession and its aftermath and the government exerted special efforts to reach veterans who might be helped by the programs.

The veterans' readjustment program is flexible in allowing the veteran his choice in selecting a program of education or training and the method of completing that program. Within broad guidelines the program offers income support and leaves to the veterans the selection of training, educational courses, and facilities. The law distinguishes between institutional education or training and on-the-job training programs. Most of the post-Korean veterans have applied their GI bill benefits to college level courses, while only a little more than one percent of the trainees have returned to high school. The others are distributed among vocational, on-the-job, and correspondence training. Farm programs have attracted less than 10,000 of the 3.1 million trainees (table 24).

Program Administration and Monitoring

The Education and Rehabilitation Service of the Department of Veterans Benefits is responsible for the administration of education and training benefits. The actual processing of applications for educational

Table 24.   *Over Three Million Veterans Enrolled in Education and*
Training Programs between 1966 and June 1972

Type of Program	Number (thousands)	Percent
Total[1]	3,066	100.0
Higher Education	*1,687*	*55.0*
Graduate	290	9.5
Undergraduate	1,366	44.6
Nondegree	23	.8
Correspondence	7	.2
Below College	*1,115*	*36.4*
Vocational and Technical	442	14.4
High School	39	1.3
Flight Training	75	2.4
Farm	9	.3
Correspondence	551	18.0
On-the-job Training	*264*	*8.6*
Apprenticeship	150	4.9
Other On-the-job Training	114	3.7

Source: U.S. Veterans Administration, *Veterans Benefits Under Current Educational Programs,* Department of Veterans Benefits Information Bulletin 24–72–6, June 1972, appendix table 3, p. 20.
Note: Details may not add to totals because of rounding.
[1] Excludes 60,000 servicemen enrolled in higher education and 207,000 in below college programs.

benefits is the responsibility of the adjudication divisions of the regional offices. Their staff members assist the veteran in choosing a program and in filing the proper application.

Consistent with its philosophy, the VA relies on existing facilities, institutions, or businesses for the education and training of veterans. Although a veteran is free to choose his own program of study, experience demonstrated that certain safeguards were necessary to assure that the veteran received responsible training and that the taxpayer's dollars were spent beneficially. The law requires that financial assistance can be awarded for enrollment only in approved courses or training programs. The right to approve courses is reserved for an appropriate state approving agency where the institution offering the program is located. The VA reimburses these state approving agencies for their services. In 1972 the VA had contracts with 69 state approval agencies at an annual cost of $8 million.

The governor of each state designates one or more approving agencies. In the states having two agencies, the most common arrangement is to assign to the department of education responsibility for approval of institutional training and the department of labor responsibility for apprenticeship and other on-the-job training. Professional accreditation associations help the approval agencies in decisions concerning the institutional courses.

After the state approving agency makes the decision on the adequacy of the quality of the courses, institutions, and training programs, final determination of whether the course of study offers a "program of education" as defined in the law rests with the VA. Although the definition is very liberal, it does exclude various recreational or avocational courses. To avoid fly-by-night institutions, the guidelines require that a proprietary school at less than the college level must have offered a course for two years before a veteran is eligible to enroll and receive benefits. Also, no more than 85 percent of the students in a nonaccredited course may be veterans.

The VA has retained the responsibility for direct approval in several instances. Schools or courses in foreign countries, training in federal agencies, and programs offered by interstate carriers such as airlines or railroads are approved by the VA rather than the state approval agencies.

It is difficult to assess the impact of these approval and monitoring measures on the quality of the programs which the veteran enters. Professional accreditation and government training standards are followed in assessing quality or adequacy, and even accreditation or minimum standards do not automatically lead to approval. Many of the institutional programs or training courses may be of questionable quality and marginal benefit to the veteran, thereby wasting the veteran's time and the public dollar. But it is certain that these safeguards assure greater protection and higher quality programs than those available to the general public where legal safeguards are minimal at most.

Generally, the institutions or establishments offering the approved programs have very little contact or relationship with the VA beyond the initial approval process. Educational institutions process veterans much as they do nonveterans and they receive a nominal reimbursement at a rate of $3 per veteran enrolled for the extra paperwork. Training establishments with on-the-job training programs must also verify monthly hours worked and wages earned, but the paperwork and mailing is handled by the veteran and there is no reimbursement.

Eligibility and Institutions

One of the paramount features of the GI bills has been their near universality in coverage of veterans. Although the present eligibility requirements are somewhat more restrictive than in the past, the concept of universal eligibility for veterans with substantial service remains intact.

As defined by the Veterans Educational Assistance Act, a veteran qualifies for benefits if he

    (1) served on active duty in the armed forces for a period of more than 180 days, any part of which occurred after January 31, 1955; or

    (2) was discharged for a service-connected disability; and

    (3) was discharged under conditions other than dishonorable.

The 181 day service requirement was designed to exclude reservists serving less than six months active duty in the armed forces.

A veteran is eligible for benefits for eight years after the date of his discharge. Exceptions are made to this general regulation for veterans who were discharged before the passage of the law in 1966 and for veterans whose discharge status has undergone a change since separation.

For each month of service a veteran is eligible to receive one and a half months of full time education or training assistance. The minimum period of service, six months, entitles a veteran to benefits for nine months. Once the period of service reaches 18 months, the veteran automatically becomes entitled to the maximum 36 months assistance.

Of the 1.2 million Vietnam era veterans receiving training allowances in April 1972, over six of ten were enrolled in institutions for higher learning (table 25). The number of Vietnam era veterans choosing to enroll in institutions of higher learning has been increasing. About one in seven of those attending institutions of higher learning were doing postgraduate work and about 40 percent attended junior or community colleges. The popularity of these colleges is largely due to the relative inexpensiveness of these schools, the proximity to the veterans' residence, and the wide variety of courses in both academic and technical training.

Veterans enrolled in some 4,800 institutions of higher learning in 1971. One-third of these were public institutions and two-thirds were private. When the number of veterans enrolled is taken into consideration, however, the ratio is reversed with almost 80 percent enrolled in public institutions. This compares with the 48 percent of World War II veterans who enrolled in public institutions. The greater availability of public institutions and the soaring costs of education in private institutions largely explain this shift.

The VA permits veterans maximum discretion in their choice of educational or training programs. The agency maintains, therefore, only casual data about the academic pursuits of enrollees. In the absence of operational needs, the VA has no records about the courses pursued by a majority of enrollees.

College level training has accounted for nearly three of every four

Table 25.   Almost 1.2 Million Veterans Were Enrolled in Education and
Training Programs under the GI Bill in April 1972

Type of Program	Number (thousands)	Percent
Total[1]	*1,164*	*100.0*
Higher Education	*748*	*64.4*
Graduate	104	8.9
Undergraduate	637	54.7
Nondegree	5	.5
Correspondence	3	.3
Below College	*319*	*27.4*
Vocational & Technical	86	7.4
High School	12	1.0
Flight Training	20	1.7
Farm	7	.6
Correspondence	194	16.7
On-the-job Training	*96*	*8.2*
Apprenticeship	61	5.2
Other On-the-job Training	35	3.0

Source: U.S. Veterans Administration, *Veterans Benefits Under Current Educational Programs,* Department of Veterans Benefits Information Bulletin 24–72–4, June 27, 1972, appendix table 1.
Note: Details may not add to totals because of roundings.
[1] Does not include 82,000 servicemen.

institutional enrollments. Over 25 percent of all veterans receiving benefits for readjustment training were enrolled in over 6,000 institutions below the college level. As in the college level program, the number of private institutions below college level that enroll veterans predominated by almost a three-to-one margin. Unlike the college program, however, the private institutions also accounted for over 85 percent of veterans enrolled, compared with 20 percent in the college program. The preference for private institutions reflects primarily the dearth of public educational or training facilities below the college level and fees and tuition costs that are frequently within the reach of veterans.

Training Courses

Vocational and technical training of veterans in below-college level training was concentrated heavily in technical, business and commerce, and trade and industrial courses (chart 22). These three areas accounted for 75 to 80 percent of all persons enrolled. Electronics technicians accounted for about four-fifths of the veterans in the technical courses. Accounting, computer technology, and real estate or

CHART 22

DISTRIBUTION OF VETERANS AND SERVICEMEN
IN BELOW COLLEGE-LEVEL COURSES , 1966-1971

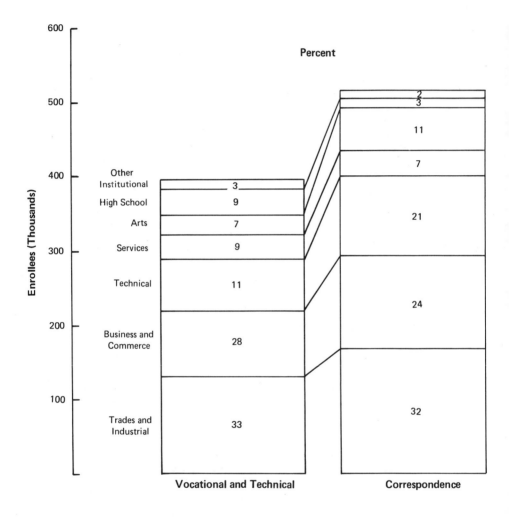

Source: U.S. Veterans Administration, *Schools Below the College Level Cumulative from June 1, 1966 through June 30, 1971* (mimeographed) and *Correspondence Courses in Schools Below College Level (Cumulative through 1971)* (mimeographed).

insurance were the major business interests (over 50 percent) and air conditioning, electronic trades, and mechanical courses (largely automotive) accounted for over three-fifths of those in trade and industrial pursuits.

These distributions indicated that veterans, to a large extent, entered courses which offer good futures. Computer technology, accounting, electronics, and automotive mechanics are generally fields where there has been and should continue to be a growing demand for labor in a tight labor market.

Of the servicemen leaving the military each year, approximately 20 percent have not completed their high school education. The VA estimates that as of June 1972 a total of 284,000 veterans and 29,000 servicemen without high school credentials entered training under the 1966 GI bill. Most entered vocational and on-the-job training courses not requiring high school completion. This is to be expected, since the VA policy of allowing the veteran a free choice in selecting his program of studies does not necessarily emphasize the importance of high school education.

Under the World War II GI bill all stipends were charges against the veterans' educational entitlement. To motivate veterans who had not completed high school, the 1970 amendments to the 1966 bill qualified them to enroll in secondary education courses without reducing their entitlement, provided they needed these courses to qualify for further training. This provision enables the veteran to complete high school and continue through four years of college work, all under the GI bill. Veterans using the so-called "free entitlement" for high school and college preparatory classes may receive payments for tutorial assistance for nine months at not more than $50 per month in addition to the regular institutional stipends. As of June 1972, some 89,000 veterans and 19,000 servicemen had taken advantage of the free entitlement. Most of the trainees were enrolled in high school courses, although some were in college, taking noncredit courses to prepare them for the standard curriculum. "Free entitlement" widens the options of educationally disadvantaged veterans and may have encouraged some of the 89,000 veterans to complete their high school education prior to embarking on a vocational career or continuing their higher education.

Correspondence Courses

Data on below-college level training must be used with considerable caution, since over 50 percent of the veterans and servicemen enrolled in this level of training have enrolled in correspondence courses of questionable merit. In fact, approximately one-sixth of all trainees have enrolled in such courses at a cost of $237 million in benefits under the current GI bill. Enrollment in these courses grew by over one-third during fiscal 1971 compared with less than a one-fifth growth in college enrollments.

Despite the popularity of correspondence courses, there are problems connected with them that have been given considerable attention. Correspondence courses must be approved by the National Home Study Council, designated by the Department of Health, Education and Welfare as the accrediting agency for such courses, or by the state approving agency of the state in which the school is located. A GAO study, however, has pointed out that accreditation does not prevent problems. The study suggested that correspondence courses may not be good investments for either the veteran's time or the public's money.[21] Of the 212,000 veterans who were no longer receiving educational assistance payments for correspondence courses at the end of fiscal 1970, some 160,000 had not completed their courses. Some dropouts reported to the GAO that the courses were too time-consuming or too difficult to be practical for them. Others said they lost interest or that the course did not fulfill their expectations. Fifty-seven percent of those who failed to complete correspondence courses stated that they would have chosen a different form of education if they had been aware before they started of the difficulties they would face in trying to complete the course of study.

Enrolling in correspondence courses can also become expensive for veterans, especially if they do not complete the course. Because the VA reimburses the enrollees in quarterly payments only for completed lessons, the veteran normally must invest his own money in advance. Responding to criticism by the GAO study, the 1972 law established a refund policy and a ten day cooling-off period for correspondence enrollees. Previously veterans dropping out of a school accredited by the National Home Study Council paid a fixed percentage of the charge for the course or a pro rata charge for the lessons completed, whichever was greater. If the course was not nationally accredited, the charge could not exceed the approximate pro rata charge of completed lessons. According to the GAO study, veterans and servicemen who dropped out of correspondence courses incurred an average cost of $180. Thirty-one percent of the dropouts did not know that the VA reimbursement would not cover their costs if they did not complete the course and most were not aware that they would have to request a refund if they were eligible for one. Veterans now have a 10 day period during which they can drop out of the course subject only to a charge of 10 percent of the cost of the course or a $50 registration fee, whichever is less. If the veteran completes less than 25 percent or less than 50 percent of the course, he must pay the registration fee plus 25 or 50 percent of the cost of the course respectively. Veterans who complete over one-half of the course before terminating receive no refund.

Refunds are not the only source of frustration to correspondence course enrollees. Information gathered by the VA showed that many veterans feel that the claims made by the sponsors of the courses that they provide adequate vocational training and employment opportunities are unfounded. Other veterans complained of the questionable business practices or even illegal activities of some sponsors. These included the use of the VA seal on promotion literature, claims that courses had "VA accreditation," and inducing the veteran to sign a loan application when he thought he was only applying for enrollment.[22]

Because the veteran's entitlement is reduced by one month for each $220 paid to him by the VA, his aggregate entitlement is reduced by pursuing a correspondence course. In order to discourage frivolous use of entitlement for correspondence courses, the 1972 law required that veterans pay 10 percent of the cost. The provision is an attempt to put the veteran in the same position as enrollees in most other institutional courses who must fund part of their own educational expenses.

Specialized Training

The law provides some specialized instruction for veterans. Farm training is available to veterans who own or manage a farm or have prospects of doing so. To be eligible for these education benefits, veterans in a farm program must take institutional courses related to farm operations in conjunction with actual farm experience. Until October 1972, a post-Korean veteran with no dependents was required to take a minimum of 12 hours of institutional training each week for 44 weeks (528 hours during the year) to be eligible to receive the full-time training stipend.

Few young veterans have turned recently to farm training. Under World War II and Korean GI bills, the participation rates for veterans in farm training were 3.6 percent and 1.7 percent respectively. In April 1972, only 0.3 percent of veterans receiving training stipends were participating in farm training. And this was almost triple the number enrolled the previous April. The decline in agricultural employment and the erosion of the community-based agricultural extension courses were largely responsible for this drastic decrease. Several farm lobbies have argued that the requirement for institutional coursework may have contributed to the decline. Although modern management and technical skills are generally recognized as necessary for the contemporary farmer, there was support in Congress and among the farm organizations for reducing the institutional training. Under the provisions of the October 1972 Readjustment Act, a full-time farm program consists of 10 hours per week for 44 weeks or 440 hours per year with no less than 80 clock hours in any 3 month period. The presumed justification for the relaxed training standards is to encourage more veterans to train in farm management and to contribute to the continuation of viable family farms, but, it is difficult to assess what part of the recent decrease in interest in farm training was due to the institutional requirements added to the 1966 law, and what part was due to a decline in agricultural employment. And it is not at all clear that the relaxed training standards will encourage family farming.

Flight training, another type of specialized training authorized by the veterans readjustment legislation, was more popular. By June 1972, 75,000 veterans had taken flight training and almost one-half of these received benefits during fiscal year 1972. To be entitled to flight training, a veteran must hold a private pilot's license and also be able to show how further flight training will help his present career or contribute to some employment objective. He can only attend a school which is approved by both the Federal Aviation Agency and the state approving agency.

Most of the veterans who enter flight training complete the course, according to the VA. Moreover, nine out of ten who complete flight training continue to take advanced courses in instrument rating and multiengines. However, the VA has not published any data about the extent that flight training serves as preparation for employment or for avocational pursuits.

On-the-Job Training

The GI bill also makes provision for training of veterans in a noninstitutional setting. In providing for veterans who seek on-the-job training, Congress has faced the perennial problem of assuring that the assistance would aid the intended clients of the program rather than subsidize employers.

As with other education benefits, on-the-job training must be approved by the state approving agency and must be designed to provide for upward occupational mobility. If a veteran desires to enter on-the-job training under an employer not approved by the state approving agency, he is free to encourage the employer to apply for approval. As a condition of approval, the wages paid by the employer to the veteran must be no less than those paid to nonveterans training for the same position and must at least equal 50 percent of the journeymen's rate. The wage schedule must also provide progression to 85 percent of the journeymen's wage prior to the completion of the training period.

In addition to the wage requirements, the training must be structured to last between six and twenty-four months. The length should be equivalent to that of comparable establishments for comparable jobs. And, finally, there must be a reasonable assurance that the target job will be available to the veteran upon completion of the training.

The state approving agency is responsible for investigating on-the-job training programs to assure that the content of the training and facilities are adequate to prepare the veteran for his job objective. The veteran is obligated to keep a record of his progress each month, which must be signed by the employer and submitted to the VA.

Apprenticeship programs for veterans must meet guidelines set by the Secretary of Labor.[23] To be "recognized," an apprenticeship program must be registered with the state approving agency or with the Bureau of Apprenticeship and Training of the Department of Labor.

Less than one-tenth of the veterans receiving education and training benefits have opted for OJT or apprenticeship (table 25). During 1972 the VA began a special outreach program to attract OJT trainees. Visits to over 100,000 employers opened over 84,000 OJT slots during the year. Although the future impact of the new effort is uncertain, it resulted in a growth in OJT enrollments over the traditionally more popular apprenticeship programs during 1972.

Education and Training Benefits

The payments made to veterans enrolled in education and training programs are in the nature of a supplemental stipend rather than a wage to support the veteran and his dependents. Having determined that the readjustment stipend is not to be considered a subsistence wage, Congress lacked any criteria for establishing a "proper" level of benefits. The amount paid to a single veteran attending full-time school prior to October 1972, the period when most of the Vietnam veterans entered civilian life, was $175 per month or less. Effective in October 1972, the basic benefit for enrollees was raised to $220 per month. Recognizing that a veteran with dependents had greater financial responsibilities and added difficulties in pursuing a course of education and training than a single veteran, Congress raised the stipend for a veteran with a single dependent to $261 a month and to $298 to a veteran with two dependents. The sipend was boosted by another $18 for each additional dependent. A veteran enrolled in an educational training program was deemed to be entitled to a full-time stipend if he attended a training program for 30 or more hours or if he was enrolled in a college for at least 14 semester hours or its equivalent. Part-time enrollees received proportionate payment. For example, a single student enrolled for 10 to 13 semester hours was entitled to three-fourths of the full-time stipend, or $165 a month. Similarly, a single veteran enrolled in 7 to 9 hours received $110 a month (table 26).

Given the arbitrary determination of allowances, comparison with benefits paid to World War II and Korean GIs was inevitable. Precise comparisons are difficult because of changed provisions. It would seem, however, that World War II veterans had a better deal than their Vietnam successors. The single World War II veteran enrolled in institutional training received a monthly allowance of $75 plus up to $500 per year for tuition paid directly to the institution in which the veteran was enrolled. The amount was adequate to cover the tuition charged at that time by most schools, and the veteran was left with his allowance.

As the cost of education rose, the VA arrangements entailed considerable burden to educational institutions, particularly publicly supported facilities. Even in private institutions, tuition does not normally cover actual costs and the students are subsidized. In the public institutions, tuition is minimal, if not token, and the students are, of course, subsidized from public revenue. The VA reimbursement under World War II arrangements, therefore, placed the burden on educational and training institutions, since the government allowances encouraged veterans to undertake education and training programs, but the VA payment did not cover the actual cost of training. Attempts to assess the costs for enrolling and training veterans proved unsuccessful and the direct payment for expenses to the school was discontinued. Instead, the government was to give the veteran a uniform allowance and left it to the trainee to pay whatever tuition the institution charged to other students.

The cash stipend paid to the Vietnam veteran, even after adjusting for changes in cost of living, still exceeded in 1972 the amounts paid to

Table 26.   Monthly Institutional Benefits

Type of Enrollment	No Dependents	One Dependent	Two Dependents	Each Additional Dependent
Full time	$220	$261	$298	$18
Three-quarter time	165	196	224	14
Half time[1]	110	131	149	9

Source: "Vietnam Era Veterans' Readjustment Assistance Act of 1972," Public Law 92–540, October 24, 1972.

[1] The allowance for veterans enrolled on less than a half-time basis or for servicemen on active duty cannot exceed the established tuition and fee charges that nonveterans pay in the same course or the above rate established at $220 for full-time, whichever is less.

the World War II and Korean veterans. Adjusted for 1972 prices, the $75 monthly payment of the World War II veteran in 1948 equalled $131. The $110 paid to the Korean veteran in 1954, adjusted for rises in cost of living, amounted to $172 and was very close to the amount received by the Vietnam veteran during most of that year. But comparing payments to the three sets of veterans should also take into consideration the overall increase in productivity and standard of living and not only cost of living. Based on these calculations it appears that society treated the World War II veteran more favorably than his successors during the two "unofficial" wars. Between 1948 and June 1972, per capita disposable income in the United States rose by 191 percent. Using this criterion, the $75 a month allowance to the single World War II veterans in 1948 should have been raised to $218 for Vietnam veterans.

Although the basic benefit for Vietnam veterans was raised to $220 in October 1972, the government did not pay any tuition for the Korean or Vietnam veteran. About three of every four Vietnam veterans enrolled in public colleges, but in 1972 they still had to pay an average annual tuition in these public institutions of $383.[24] This tuition, subtracted from the $1,575 annual stipend (based on a nine-month school year), left the veteran with about $130 a month while he was attending school. A veteran who chose to attend a private school had to pay an average tuition fee of $255 in excess of the total allowance he received from the government; the average tuition in private schools in 1972 was $1,830. Receiving increased benefits and paying more tuition, veterans in public schools will be somewhat better off during 1973. Paying an average tuition of $392 out of $1,980 in allowances will leave him $188 per month. The veteran in a private school will receive benefits only slightly greater than his $1,919 tuition bill.

The above calculations do not consider, however, the duration of benefits, which tend to favor Vietnam veterans. World War II veterans received one month of educational allowances for each month served on active duty, up to 48 months. Because most served lengthy tours of duty, they qualified for maximum benefits. Vietnam and Korean veterans were entitled to 1.5 months of educational allowances for each month of service and those serving 18 months have been eligible for the maximum entitlement of 36 months, giving them time to complete the normal college course.

The Vietnam veteran enrolled in a college or institutional training was in a position to pyramid benefits and some did. Funds are available under the Education Professions Development Act, the Educational Talent Search, Careers Opportunities Program and Teacher Corps to those pursuing postsecondary education in the fields of elementary, high school, and college teaching, administration, and counseling. Since March 1970 veterans have been eligible to receive GI bill education benefits concurrent with federal followship aid. During fiscal year 1972, the Office of Education estimated that a little over $17 million would be spent to assist approximately 4,500 veterans in these programs.[25] In addition, other veterans received Equal Opportunity Grants, College Work Study, National Defense Education Act Student Loans, or Guaranteed Student Loans to support their college training.

The veteran who chooses institutional noncollege training may be no better off than the one who attends college. Duration of training and costs of vocational and technical training vary widely. In order to qualify for full-time benefits of $220 a month, the veteran would have to attend upwards of 100 hours of training. The tuition fee alone would therefore about equal the total allowances received by the veteran. As with college students, vocational and technical trainees must bear the costs of books and supplies as well as living expenses.

A modest work-study provision added in the 1972 law offers assistance to veterans who cannot meet the full costs of their education. Funding is limited to approximately 16,000 veterans at a cost of $4 million each year. A needy veteran can receive up to $250 in advance for agreeing to work 100 hours for the VA. Not only is the program intended to help veterans who need part-time work during the school year, but it also assists the VA regional offices in their outreach efforts to aid other veterans, the processing of paperwork for the education program, or for work in VA medical facilities.

Another 1972 provision to ease the financial burden on the veteran at the beginning of the school terms was the advance payment of educational assistance allowances to cover costs of books, supplies, and registration fees. A veteran who is at least a half-time student can receive the amount due him during the month he starts school plus the following month's stipend. During subsequent months the veteran receives prepaid allowances as long as he submits proof of enrollment and satisfactory progress. Part-time students enrolled for less than half time can receive a lump sum allowance for the term after certification of enrollment is received.

The World War II experience provided only a negative guideline for the payment of benefits for on-the-job training (OJT). The initial GI bill of 1944 imposed a limit on the earnings of veterans in on-the-job training. While in training, a single veteran was allowed a maximum monthly income of $210, including both OJT payments and wages. The stipend paid to the veteran for a maximum of two years did not affect his income since it was reduced by an amount equal to every increase in his wages. When his monthly wages reached $210, he was disqualified from receiving further allowances. The arrangement robbed the veteran of incentives to secure higher wages and frequently ended up as a subsidy to the employer rather than as a supplement to the veteran.

To remedy this situation, the 1955 law provided Korean veterans with a $70 per month allowance which was reduced at regular four month intervals, anticipating periodic increases in the trainee's wages. The ceiling on monthly income was removed, to allow veterans to press for wage increases due them. The present law requires that employers pay veterans the same wage rate as they pay nonveterans for the same job and that they pay at least the federal minimum wage of $1.60 per hour. For post-Korean veterans, OJT payments are reduced at six month intervals (table 27).

The OJT allowance serves, therefore, as an incentive for the veteran to undertake training by supplementing his income during the period of training. Since his income from apprenticeship may be below what he could get on the open market for another job, the allowance serves to compensate the veteran for earnings deferred as a result of undertaking training. Though data are not available, the allowance may also provide an incentive to the employer to hire veterans, since the lure of higher wages elsewhere frequently encourages trainees or apprentices to drop out before completing their formal course of training. The wage supplement provided by the government to the veteran may encourage more stable employment prospects.

While the 1972 law effected a 25.7 percent increase in the basic allowance paid to veterans studying in institutional and farm programs, the increase in the basic on-the-job training benefit was 48.1 percent. This increase represents an attempt to correct a traditional bias favoring institutional programs of study. Under the provisions effective between 1970 and 1972, a single on-the-job trainee working 40 hours per week all year could earn approximately $4,500 per year in wages and allowances even if his wages were not increased after the

Table 27.   *Monthly On-the-Job and Apprenticeship Benefits*

Period	No Dependents	One Dependent	Two Dependents	Each Additional Dependent
1st 6 months	$160	$179	$196	$8
2nd 6 months	120	139	156	8
3rd 6 months	80	99	116	8
4th 6 months and succeeding periods	40	52	76	8

Source: "Vietnam Era Veterans' Readjustment Assistance Act of 1972," Public Law 92–540, October 24, 1972.

first six months. The new provision will raise the annual income of the same trainee above $5,000 ($3,328 in wages and $1,680 in allowances). A married veteran with two dependents would receive almost $5,500 a year.

Little is known about the quality of training offered to veterans under OJT. In the absence of hard data it may be surmised that some employers misused the allowance system to hire veterans at lower wages. Also the OJT programs are not required to include a minimum number of employees or to have been in business for two years before receiving approval. Such loose requirements do little to assure meaningful training. However, the employer's certification that there is "reasonable certainty" that the veteran will have a job after being trained and that his wages during the last six months of training will be 85 percent of the job for which he is being trained are generally thought to assure that the training will pay off in employment for the veteran.

Costs of Training

Except for the amounts paid in veterans' benefits each year, little information is available on the expenditures involved in administering educational readjustment for veterans. The average stipend paid to each veteran enrolled for training during 1972 was $972, a small increase over the two preceding years (table 28). Most of the increase each year is due to the increasing proportion of full-time enrollees—from 48 percent in April 1970 to 59 percent in April 1972. Another factor was the slight increase (from 39 percent in April 1970 to 43 percent two years later) in the percentage of enrollees with dependents. Longer periods of training and the rising costs of flight training and correspondence courses were other additions to the increased costs. Further increases are anticipated with boosts in the level of benefits. Higher education absorbed 72 percent of the total outlays in 1972, though college students accounted for only 56 percent of enrollment. Veterans attending college were paid an average of $1,233 per student, compared with $598 received by the trade and technical students. The differences in payments were due to the fact that the vast majority of trade school enrollees qualified for only part-time or correspondence course payments while most college students received full-time stipends. In contrast, the average amount spent on educationally disadvantaged veterans was only $390. These educationally disadvantaged veterans were those using the "free entitlement" to take refresher courses. The $390 payment represented only the initial investment in their training, since they were expected to move into college and vocational courses during succeeding years.

*Table 28.   Outlays for Veteran Education and Training Programs
           Exceeded $1.8 Billion in 1972*

Type of Training	Number of Trainees	Unit Cost	Total Cost (thousands)
Total	1,864,158	$ 972	$1,812,434
Higher Education			
Graduate	170,359	1,101	187,650
Undergraduate	894,154	1,258	1,124,869
Junior College	(389,900)	(1,169)	(455,742)
Other Education			
High School	39,973	420	16,789
Trade or Technical	546,458	558	305,081
On-Job	161,683	734	118,623
Flight	42,647	1,029	43,893
Cooperative Farm	8,884	1,748	15,529
Educationally Disadvantaged	(67,201)	(390)	(26,208)
Servicemen	(139,908)	(345)	(48,308)
Correspondence	(282,292)	(396)	(111,754)

Source: U.S. Veterans Administration, Management and Budget Service, unpublished table prepared October 31, 1972.

Note: Figures in parenthesis are not added to the total, as they are included in other items.

Trainee Characteristics

More than half the Vietnam trainees were 25 years or older—an age when most other adults are already set on a career. The "advanced" age of the veteran trainee reflects the two years or more "lost" in the service, and the special inducements the government offers to the veteran may attract young adults to return to school.

The typical trainee graduated from high school prior to entering service. The veterans who had dropped out of school prior to graduation from high school have tended to take less advantage of the education and training benefits than veterans with a high school education. While one of every five veterans had failed to graduate from high school, only 8 percent of the veterans enrolled in education or training programs had less than a high school education (chart 23). A study of all enlisted reservists—two of every three persons separated—for the three-year period ending in 1971 disclosed that 34.5 percent entered some form of training or educational program. The participation rate was highest for veterans who had some college education prior to entering service but who had not graduated. Those with less than a high school education prior to entering the service had the lowest participation rate.

Participation rates of blacks were lower than for whites. While more than one of every three whites received educational training

CHART 23

THE MOST DEFICIENTLY EDUCATED VETERANS TENDED NOT TO ENROLL
IN GI BILL PROGRAMS
(CUMULATIVE TO JUNE 1972)

Education Level

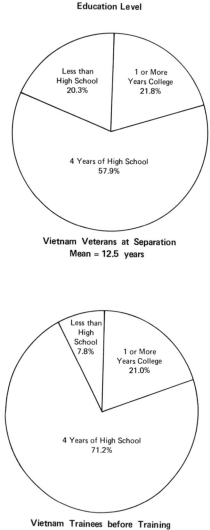

Vietnam Veterans at Separation
Mean = 12.5 years

Vietnam Trainees before Training
Mean = 12.6 years

Source: Figures for All Vietnam Veterans: U.S. Veterans Administration, Reports and Statistics
Service, *Data on Vietnam Era Veterans*, June 1972, p. 7.

Figures for Vietnam Trainees: U.S. Veterans Administration, *Veterans Benefits Under
Current Educational Programs,* Department of Veterans Benefits Information Bulletin
24-72-6, June 1972, p. 32.

benefits, only one-fourth of the blacks participated in these programs. Except for those with less than a high school education, the proportion of blacks who received education and training benefits was lower in every other educational category than for that of whites. It would seem that the traditional "color blind" policy of VA has not resulted in blacks reaping their proportion of GI bill benefits (chart 24).

The lower participation rates of the deficiently educated and black veterans in the GI bill may also reflect a bias inherent in the legislation. The law favors those attending college as compared with those participating in technical or vocational training. The veteran who is attending a college course receives benefits for full-time training for the minimal number of hours which is considered a full-time course load at that institution. The veteran who is enrolled in a technical or vocational program, however, must meet weekly course hour requirements and is subjected to a more stringent reporting procedure attest-

CHART 24

BLACKS WERE REPRESENTED LESS THAN WHITES IN GI BILL PROGRAMS
(THOSE WHO SEPARATED BETWEEN JULY 1, 1968, AND DECEMBER 31, 1970)

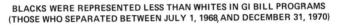

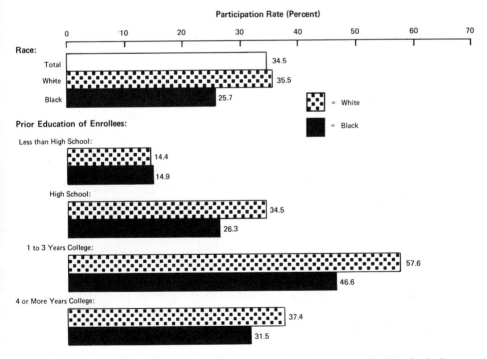

Source: Human Resources Research Organization, "DOD Post-Service Analysis of Men Separating 1 July 1968–31 December 1970" (unpublished).

ing to his attendance. The college student is given considerable leeway to augment his income, since a schedule of 14 credit hours is considered full-time work and that permits the student to seek part-time employment. The veteran enrolled in a vocational or technical course must, however, attend institutional training for at least 25 and sometimes 30 hours a week in order to qualify for full time allowances.[26] The inequity becomes apparent in the case of two veterans enrolled in the same classes but with different degree objectives. Both veterans may be enrolled in mathematics and electronics courses, but the veteran enrolled for a degree has to be enrolled in 14 credit hours in order to get his full benefits while the veteran who takes these courses in order to qualify for, say, electronics equipment repair, does not qualify for full-time benefits unless he has at least a 25-hour schedule of institutional training.

VA participation data clearly indicate a rising emphasis on college education under the GI bill. Less than one of every three World War II veterans who participated in training was enrolled in college, compared with nearly six of ten post-Korean veterans (chart 25). The lower enrollment rate of the high school dropout may reflect the lack of interest in added formal education or skill training, but it may also reflect the biases in the law which tend to offer him less benefits than the degree-bound student. Also, the counseling offered to most veterans is inadequate to formulate a career education plan and veterans frequently gravitate to college courses without a clear vocational objective.

It may be questioned whether the bias in favor of the degree-bound college student matches societal needs. A strong case can be made that a greater need exists in the post-Vietnam United States for skilled craftsmen and that higher, or more exactly, longer education has been oversold. Inexorable laws of supply and demand may indeed prove that by further stimulating the supply of college-trained persons in the labor force, the GI bill has helped to devalue the worth of a sheepskin while societal needs were greater for the training of skilled craftsmen or technicians, which was not encouraged by the law.

Federal Manpower Programs

Federally-supported manpower programs are another option open to veterans seeking vocational training. These received little attention as choices for veterans until the President announced his veterans' program in June 1971. In the past, the major thrust of manpower programs has been to train disadvantaged individuals and to assist them in finding employment. Beginning in March 1972, however, Vietnam veterans were given absolute preference in all programs, ex-

CHART 25

THE PROPORTION OF VETERANS ENROLLING IN COLLEGE UNDER THE GI BILL
DOUBLED SINCE WORLD WAR II

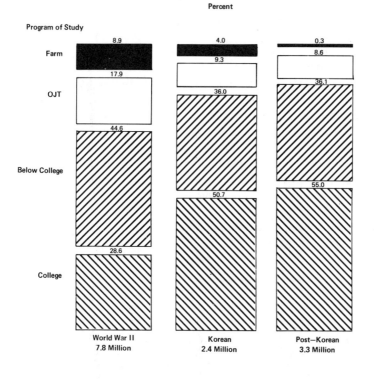

Percent

Program of Study

	World War II 7.8 Million	Korean 2.4 Million	Post–Korean 3.3 Million
Farm	8.9	4.0	0.3
OJT	17.9	9.3	8.6
Below College	44.6	36.0	36.1
College	28.6	50.7	55.0

Source: U.S. Veterans Administration, *Veterans Benefits Under Current Educational Programs,* Department of Veterans Benefits Information Bulletin 24-72-6, June 1972, p. 30.

cept for those limited to unemployed and low income persons under the Economic Opportunity Act.[27] As a result, all veterans who desired training, not just the disadvantaged, could enroll in federally-supported programs. The options offered to veterans in the various federally-funded manpower programs are not insignificant. According to the Department of Labor, almost 150,000 Vietnam veterans entered manpower programs during 1972.

Whether the "absolute" preference accorded veterans will remain rhetoric or add viable options for veterans seeking vocational training remains to be seen. Veterans were attracted to the Public Employment Program funded under the Emergency Employment Act. The Labor Department has estimated that over 60,000 Vietnam veterans were placed in state and local jobs under this program. But these were real jobs paying established wage and salary rates. Veterans apparently found the training programs less attractive. Despite the priority they received, only some 40,000 Vietnam veterans enrolled in Manpower Development and Training Act institutional programs during 1972, although possibly five times as many enrolled in "less than college" training supported by the GI bill during the year.

Although 40,000 veterans enrolled in MDTA-Institutional training and another 18,000 enrolled in on-the-job training sponsored by the Department of Labor, not all were able to collect GI bill benefits. The average MDTA training stipends of almost $225 per month, added to the basic GI bill benefit of $220 each month, would appear to be a substantial incentive for veterans seeking below college institutional training. However, some MDTA courses are contracted with private institutions which do not meet the VA requirement of having been in existence for two years. Federally-supported on-the-job training programs of less than six months duration and which do not assure a reasonable certainty of providing a job also do not conform to VA standards. Some 15,000 veterans did enroll in Department of Labor apprenticeship programs for which the standards are generally the same for both agencies.

The Disabled Veteran—A Special Case

Throughout American history, society has felt a pressing responsibility to the veteran disabled in military service. During the post-World War I period, disabled veterans were singled out for readjustment benefits. Within the decade after the end of the war over 675,000 veterans applied for vocational rehabilitation, of whom one-half were found eligible. The VA claimed that of the 180,000 disabled veterans who eventually entered training, 129,000 successfully completed their courses. Two-thirds of the trainees were equally distributed in institutional and on-the-job training programs and the remaining one-third participated in a combination of both types of training.[28]

The presumed successes of the World War I program paved the way for a similar program for later disabled veterans. It established the feasibility of vocational rehabilitation through education and training. Moreover, the accomplishments of the educational program for disabled veterans were factors in the decision to provide all World War II veterans with education and training benefits.

The vocational rehabilitation program for disabled World War II veterans began in 1943. All servicemen with a disability of 10 percent or more were eligible. One year later education benefits for the non-disabled were approved. Over 600,000 disabled World War II veterans, or 27 percent of those with a service-connected disability, entered vocational rehabilitation. Another 400,000 disabled veterans were counseled, but did not enter the program.[29] Because vocational rehabilitation study plans were subject to a continuing monitoring by a vocational counselor, it is probable that many other disabled veterans chose their own educational programs under the regular GI bill benefits.

Under a 1950 law, veterans disabled during the Korean conflict were provided basically the same vocational rehabilitation benefits as World War II veterans. Later, in 1962, the benefits were extended to peacetime and Vietnam veterans. However, only those whose disability was rated at 30 percent or over were covered by the law.

Administration

Every honorably discharged veteran who receives compensation for a disability may be considered for vocational rehabilitation. The Medical Policy Board in each VA regional office has the responsibility for determining the degree of the veteran's disability and his eligibility for compensation payments. As in the case of nondisabled veterans, the adjudication division must establish his entitlement for vocational rehabilitation. But unlike the program for nondisabled veterans, his entitlement and enrollment in vocational rehabilitation must have a particular employment objective as its goal. For those with disability ratings of 30 percent and above, the "pronounced employment handicap" necessary to gain entitlement is presumed to exist. However, the guideline is flexible enough to allow the vocational counselor to deny benefits to some veterans with a greater than 30 percent disability if he determines that vocational rehabilitation is unnecessary. On the other hand, the counselor may qualify veterans whose lesser disabilities constitute employment handicaps.

Vocational rehabilitation is denied in few cases. Of the 20,500 veterans for whom counseling was completed during 1971, only 2,560 were denied training. Most were men with a disability rating under 30 percent. Those denied vocational rehabilitation are then assisted in entering a regular GI bill program of studies.

When any doubt exists concerning the medical feasibility of training a severely disabled veteran, his case is referred to the regional office's Vocational Rehabilitation Board. The board, which is composed of personnel who specialize in counseling, training, and adjustment, helps in planning a integrated program of services—counseling, medical, and vocational—for the veteran.

Eligibility for most World War II veterans ended in 1956 and for peacetime veterans who served before 1962 the cut-off was 1971. Post-

Korean veterans are eligible to enroll in vocational rehabilitation during the 9 years following their release from active duty. However, extensions up to four years are possible if medical problems have delayed
the beginning of training, if compensable disability was not established
within the normal time period, or if a dishonorable discharge was
subsequently changed, establishing the veteran's eligibility. During
1972, only 1,200 World War II and Korean veterans were among the
31,600 vocational rehabilitation trainees. Disabled Vietnam veterans
accounted for 24,800 participants. During their 9 to 13 year period of
eligibility, veterans are normally limited to four years of vocational
rehabilitation, although exceptions can be made to lengthen the program for men whose health deteriorates or who need several different
types of training at different times.

Outreach and Intake

The VA attempts to locate disabled veterans and motivate them to
enroll in vocational rehabilitation as early as possible. Both the military
and VA hospitals have psychologists available to counsel disabled patients. In addition, VA counselors from the regional offices visit these
hospitals to begin the process of determining an education or training
plan for the disabled serviceman or veteran. Those men who are not
reached while in the hospital are contacted after applying for disability
compensation. Copies of all disability ratings are passed on to vocational
rehabilitation counselors who contact the veterans to offer VA services.

During the course of counseling and establishing an education or
training plan, disabled veterans receive more intensive attention than
those applying for regular GI bill benefits. Aptitude and interest tests
are normally administered along with motor ability tests to assure that
a suitable occupation is chosen and that any additional physical
restoration required is undertaken.

To assure as complete a coverage as possible of those disabled
veterans eligible for VA benefits, the VA staff cooperates with the state
vocational rehabilitation agencies. When a veteran eligible for VA
benefits approaches a state agency for assistance he is referred to the
VA in order to exhaust VA services and his vocational rehabilitation
entitlement before turning to the state agency for help. Although it is
not frequently necessary, the VA can work with state agencies on behalf of veterans who reach the end of their 9 to 13 year period of
eligibility without completing their rehabilitation, to assure that the
federal-state agencies will continue to aid the victims for the remainder
of their program. Other disabled veterans who are not entitled to VA
vocational rehabilitation, for example those with no service-connected

handicaps, are referred to the state agency where they can receive assistance.

Benefits

Unlike the nondisabled veteran who receives only a stipend during his period of training, the costs of training and education of the disabled veteran are fully covered by the government. In addition, the veteran receives a subsistence allowance during his rehabilitation and for two months after completion (table 29). Under the 1972 law the basic benefit to a single veteran in vocational rehabilitation was $170 per month. The 26 percent increase which became effective in October 1972 was comparable to other increases for nondisabled veterans, except for veterans pursuing vocational rehabilitation in on-the-job training.

Hospitalized servicemen who enter vocational rehabilitation prior to their discharge are ineligible for subsistence allowances. The total of the stipend plus the wages of a disabled veteran in on-the-job training is limited to the base pay of a fully trained journeyman. When the trainee's total income exceeds that amount his stipend is cut accordingly.

The veteran qualifying for vocational rehabilitation is not likely to get rich while participating in the program, but the financial benefits appear adequate to maintain the veteran until he can work again. Since most are qualified for at least a 30 percent disability compensation, the combined monthly income under the 1972 law for most single veterans in an institutional program was $247, none of which had to be applied to the costs of training. Tuition, fees, books, sup-

Table 29. Disabled Veterans Receive Monthly Subsistence Allowances in Addition to Training Costs

Type of Training	No Dependents	One Dependent	Two Dependents	Each Additional Dependent
Institutional				
Full time	$170	$211	$248	$18
Three-quarter time	128	159	187	14
Half time	85	106	124	9
Farm, Apprenticeship or other				
On-the-job training				
Full time	148	179	207	14

Source: "Vietnam Era Veterans' Readjustment Assistance Act of 1972," Public Law 92–540, October 24, 1972.

plies, and equipment necessary for the program of study are covered by VA funds. A disabled veteran enrolled in OJT received a total of $225 in compensation and stipends plus whatever wages he earned.

Disabled Veteran in Training

Since the beginning of the vocational rehabilitation program in 1918, over 900,000 disabled veterans have entered training as follows:

World War I	180,000
World War II	621,000
Korean Conflict	77,000
Post-Korean peacetime period	24,000
Vietnam	44,000

Data from the first five years of the Vietnam era show that the typical disabled veteran in a vocational rehabilitation program was under 30 years old, had at least one dependent, and had at least a high school education. As was true of his predecessor from World War II and the Korean Conflict, his disability was likely to be due to an orthopedic problem or a mental disorder. In only 14 percent of the cases was impairment less than 30 percent. Almost four of ten vocational rehabilitation enrollees had disabilities rated at 30 or 40 percent and another two of ten were totally disabled.

Disabled veterans normally receive their training in the same institutions, on-the-job sites, and farm courses as the nondisabled. Like other veterans, a greater proportion of disabled Vietnam veterans have turned to colleges and universities than disabled veterans from previous periods (table 30). Six of ten disabled Vietnam veterans chose to undertake vocational rehabilitation in college, compared with approximately one-fourth of the World War II and one-third of the Korean disabled veterans.

Table 30.   Proportionately More Disabled Vietnam Veterans Enrolled in College-Level Training by June 1972 than Veterans from Previous Periods

Type of Training	World War II	Korea	Post-Korean Peacetime	Vietnam
Total	*621,000*	*77,000*	*24,000*	*44,000*
Percent	100.0	100.0	100.0	100.0
College	24.6	32.2	43.8	61.9
Below college	24.8	47.3	49.9	32.7
On-the-job training	38.3	16.2	5.7	5.0
Farm	12.3	4.3	0.6	0.4

Source: U.S. Veterans Administration, *Veterans Benefits Under Current Educational Programs,* Department of Veterans Benefits Information Bulletin 24–72–6, June 1972, p. 35.

The institutional courses in which disabled veterans have enrolled during the post-Korean period vary greatly. College programs in
education, administrative specialities, and managerial skills were most
popular. Below college institutional trainees frequently have chosen
employment goals in such professional and technical fields as administration, drafting, and technical occupations, in clerical and sales work,
or in such trade and industrial occupations as mechanics, repair, and
assembly.[30]

The decline in the proportion of veterans enrolling in on-the-job
training has been even more dramatic among those in vocational
rehabilitation programs than among regular GI bill trainees. After
World War II over one-third of the vocational rehabilitation enrollees
were training on-site, compared with only 5 percent of Vietnam era
trainees.

Since counseling on a career choice is an integral part of the
vocational rehabilitation process, it can only be concluded that more
disabled veterans are seeking and being encouraged to choose institutional courses leading to professional, technical, and managerial types
of jobs. Most of the disabled OJT trainees are working at trade and
industrial jobs, where on-site training predominates. The sites, however, are usually in small businesses or shops or in the government,
where special work conditions can more readily be adapted for the
veteran.

Because the emphasis is to insure that the vocational rehabilitation received by disabled veterans is fully vocational, special programs
have been developed for severely disabled veterans whose handicaps
prevent them from beginning an institutional or regular on-the-job
training program immediately. These special services include restorative training, remedial education, placement in sheltered workshops,
and homebound training. During fiscal 1971 approximately 800 disabled veterans were in these programs.

Special adjustment programs, such as mobility training and braille
lessons for blind veterans, are provided where possible by the VA
Department of Medicine and Surgery, although veterans can use other
special rehabilitation facilities outside the VA. Remedial education is
provided to those disabled veterans who need it in order to enter a
trade, technical, or college program. Some disabled veterans in need
of a protective setting as a transition to a normal work site are placed
in sheltered workshops. Licensed by the Department of Labor, these
public and private workshops are not required to meet VA on-the-job
training requirements. Goodwill Industries, where employees repair
items for resale, is a typical sheltered workshop. Although in some
cases sheltered workshops provide extended or terminal employment,
the VA attempts to place disabled veterans there only until their self-

confidence and skills have improved sufficiently to move on to on-the-job or institutional training. None of these types of special restorative training is considered a vocational rehabilitation program by itself. They are only steps to insure the disabled veteran will successfully complete his training or education and be placed in a permanent job.

Another special program is homebound training for severely disabled but intellectually capable veterans who can undertake a training course only in their homes. Not only medical obstacles, but motivational problems must be overcome in the case of a homebound veteran. Training is conducted for these men as long as it is medically feasible. Most often the homebound veteran who undertakes vocational rehabilitation develops a skilled trade or profession, such as repair work or accounting, which he can develop into a small business. During 1971, 250 homebound veterans were being trained.

Participation in Vocational Rehabilitation

As of June 30, 1972, there were 308,800 disabled Vietnam veterans receiving disability compensation, of whom 137,000 had a 30 percent or greater disability, the usual cut-off point for eligibility. However, not all of the 44,000 disabled Vietnam veterans who had entered vocational rehabilitation were classified disabled 30 percent or more. The participation rate in vocational rehabilitation as of mid-1972 was therefore less than 30 percent, somewhat lower than among the nondisabled GI bill trainees. It may not be meaningful to compare participation rates of the two groups, since little is known about the total need for rehabilitation among the disabled or their ability to participate. Many of the less disabled may not require vocational training, but need only help in finding a job. Also, there may be some among the 23,000 100 percent disabled who cannot participate.

More important in measuring the success of the vocational rehabilitation program is the proportion of men taking vocational rehabilitation who are rehabilitated. Since follow-up studies are not available, the only measure provided by the VA is the proportion of the World War II and Korean Conflict trainees who completed their program of education or training and were placed in jobs for which they were trained. According to this criterion, 61 percent were rehabilitated.[31] Not included among the rehabilitated are those who dropped out of the program to accept jobs. Because so many post-Korean disabled veterans are still in training, it is difficult to estimate how many will be totally rehabilitated. During fiscal year 1971, 4,280 disabled veterans completed training and 90 percent of them found jobs in the fields for which they were trained.

Some problems do exist, however, among those enrolled in vocational rehabilitation. Although some 31,600 disabled veterans were enrolled in a vocational rehabilitation program during fiscal year 1972, only 20,800 were in training in April, the peak month of the school year. Part of the difference may be due to the exit of some rehabilitated veterans. Other disabled veterans who locate employment opportunities while in training prefer to take advantage of the security of a job and abandon their training. They are not counted as rehabilitated. Others are rehospitalized and must drop out of training. Those who drop out, regardless of the reason, must apply for a redetermination of their entitlement before they can reenter the rehabilitation program.

Cost of Vocational Rehabilitation

World War I vocational rehabilitation is estimated to have cost $645 million. The comparable bill for World War II to June 1971 has totalled $421 million, coupled with over $1.5 billion in subsistence allowances.

At an average cost of about $2,000 per enrollee, the total direct cost of the veterans' vocational rehabilitation program during fiscal year 1972 was over $60 million. Subsistence allowances averaged $1,300 per trainee and the balance was allocated to the cost of training. These direct costs, however, represent only the most visible part of the expenditures to readjust disabled veterans to civilian life. The VA has apparently never attempted to analyze the indirect costs of the program. Medical expenditures and compensation payments for disabled veterans, although not defined as readjustment outlays, are necessary to guarantee that the disabled veteran is restored to a complete life.

To support the vocational rehabilitation program, for example, the VA supports some 280 counseling psychologists and 180 vocational rehabilitation specialists in its regional offices. The total cost of payroll and overhead, including support staff, added about $20,000 per employee, or another $9.6 million to the vocational rehabilitation bill.

The special restorative programs and remedial education, in which some 400 disabled veterans were enrolled during 1971, are additional costs incurred before the veteran formally begins his vocational rehabilitation. No estimate of the cost of these programs is available. Hospitalization, medical care, and prosthesis necessary to complete their training are available to vocational rehabilitation participants whether or not they would be authorized under other VA regulations. The medical expenses for restorative programs and for medical care for the disabled while in training are included in the Department of Medicine and Surgery's budget and are not computed separately for vocational rehabilitation trainees. Remedial education is also not listed as a separate expense.

Additional minor assistance is also offered. The VA maintains, for example, a revolving loan fund for disabled veterans in vocational rehabilitation. Until October 1972 a trainee could borrow up to $100 as an "advance" to be repaid interest-free; the amount was increased to $200 under the 1972 law. Some $351,000 was borrowed from the fund in 1971, and almost an equal amount was repaid.

Other Readjustment Benefits for the Disabled

Disabled veterans are the beneficiaries of several other forms of readjustment assistance that are not related directly to the costs of rehabilitation. Under a program established in 1946, veterans receiving compensation for the loss of a hand or foot or serious impairment of vision are eligible to receive assistance in purchasing an automobile or other conveyance along with the necessary adaptive equipment. As of January 1971 the basic allowance was raised from $1,600 to $2,800 for purchase of the vehicle and the installation, maintenance, repair, and replacement of the adaptive equipment. As of June 1971, over 62,000 disabled veterans had taken advantage of the program, at a cost of $101.2 million. Moreover, since 1948 paraplegic veterans have received assistance in constructing suitable housing, including the special facilities required by the disability. The maximum amount of the grant in 1972 was $17,500. It could be used to cover up to 50 percent of the cost of land and construction. By June 1972, over 12,000 such grants had been made at a cost of $120.7 million.

Readjustment benefits for disabled veterans extend beyond the VA. While the VA's vocational rehabilitation specialists are responsible for following the vocational rehabilitation trainee through his program of studies, culminating with helping to place him in a job, the specialists depend heavily on the placement offices of the training institutions, the United States Employment Service (USES) and the Civil Service Commission for help. While the USES has traditionally given preference to veterans, the disabled receive top priority under the law. The Civil Service Commission gives the disabled veteran an additional 10 points on his examination score instead of the 5 points for other veterans.

In all federal manpower programs in which veterans have priority in enrolling, disabled veterans are the first selected. Finally, disabled veterans, seeking to exercise their remployment rights and not qualified to perform their former duties due to their disabilities, are entitled to another position in the same company that will provide them similar seniority, status, and pay.

The disabled veteran is considered by the VA to be a special case most worthy of extra help and attention. As one VA official stated,

"The Congress has never refused anything for direct benefits; there are
no budget constraints. We are not even told to take only 'calculated
risks' in attempting the vocational rehabilitation of disabled veterans."
As for the indirect costs of the program for the VA and the expenditures by the state social rehabilitation services, United States Employment Service, and the Civil Service Commission, it is safe to conclude
that all reasonable efforts are made to restore the disabled veteran's
employability.

Housing and Other Loans

The GI bill offers assistance to veterans to purchase homes and
farms. This aid can be differentiated from the other direct benefits as
"deferred readjustment" because few veterans take advantage of the
housing loan program shortly after release. The program dates back to
the 1944 GI bill, which established a program of guaranteed, insured,
and direct loans to veterans to purchase or improve a home or farm or
to finance a business. Similar loan programs were extended to Korean
veterans. The home loan guaranty attracted the largest proportion of
veterans and has been the nucleus of the program since its inception.
When VA loan benefits were extended to post-Korean veterans in
1966, only home and farm loans were included in the program for
them.

Although the VA loan program was originally intended to be an
aid in the veterans' readjustment from military to civilian life, the
1970 law which eliminated the termination dates for eligibility has
rendered the program a permanent veterans' benefit. As of mid-1972,
approximately 38 percent of eligible World War II veterans and 44
percent of eligible Korean veterans had participated in the loan program. Normally, a veteran does not turn to the VA for loan assistance
until several years after his release from active duty—until he finishes
school, locates a job, and marries. Only 10 percent of the post-Korean
veterans had used the program as of June 1972. Some 20 million veterans or their dependents remain eligible for loan benefits, over and
above the 8.5 million veterans who have taken part in one of the loan
programs.

Guaranteed or Insured Loans

Veterans who desire to purchase homes can make arrangements
with the lender of their choice. The VA guarantees 60 percent of the
home loan or $12,500, whichever is less, against default. The extent of
the guaranty declines as the loan is repaid, since the VA guaranty is a
fixed percentage of the outstanding amount of the loan. The maximum
rate of interest is set by the VA to be competitive with the market rate.

It cannot exceed the FHA rate, but is normally equal to it. The VA also contracts with private appraisers to determine the reasonable value of the property, above which no guaranty coverage will be extended. The veteran may pay more than the reasonable value if he pays in cash.

Guarantees on business real estate and on nonreal estate, for which World War II and Korean veterans remain eligible, cover up to either 50 percent of the loan or up to $4,000 on real estate or $2,000 on other purchases. Only 3 percent of the loan guarantees undertaken by the VA as of the end of fiscal 1972 were business loans. Since the law was never updated to allow competitive rates of interest and larger loans, the VA business loan program is no longer attractive to veterans or to lenders.

Veterans are eligible for two types of farm loan guarantees. The first, a farm-residence loan, parallels the home loan guaranty program. The second is a guaranteed loan to purchase or improve land, livestock, equipment, or stock in a cooperative. The guaranty limits are the same as on business loans. Since the amounts of the farm-business loans are small, it is not surprising that few such loans are guaranteed each year. A more important program for veteran farmers is the loan service of the Farmers Home Administration of the Department of Agriculture, which provides loans to purchase real estate and for operating expenses. Veterans receive preference where funds are limited under this program and priority in the processing of their applications.

As of the end of fiscal 1972, 8.1 million guaranteed or insured loans had been made, with a VA initial liability of $46.8 billion on loans totaling $90.2 billion (table 31). Over 95 percent of the loans were for homes. In 1971 the average VA-guaranteed home buyer had a monthly income of $733 after taxes, of which he paid $241 for housing expenses—repayment on his loan plus taxes, insurance, and maintenance. The average purchase price of a new house was $25,100 and of

Table 31.   Most VA Loan Activity Involves Homes for Veterans
(Cumulative to June 30, 1972)

Type of Loan	Volume (thousands)	Amount (billions)
Total	8,455	$93.2
Guaranteed or Insured Loans	8,141	90.2
Home	7,841	89.2
Farm	71	.3
Business	229	.7
Direct Loans	314	3.0

Source: U.S. Veterans Administration, Loan Guaranty Service, June 30, 1972 (unpublished data).

an existing home was $21,400. Over seven of ten homebuyers made no
down payment and nine of ten negotiated mortgages of 25 to 30 years.[32]

Direct Loan Program

The VA also administers a direct loan program for veterans who
are unable to arrange a private loan due to a shortage of housing
credit in their area. A veteran may only use a direct loan to purchase,
improve, or refinance a home or farmhouse. The maximum loan is
generally $21,000, except in high-cost areas, where $25,000 is the limit.
The amount is reduced for veterans who have used a portion of their
entitlement for a guaranteed loan.

The VA acts as the lender in the case of direct loans. As in the
case of guaranteed loans, the rate and reasonable value of the property
are set by the VA. Direct loans which are sold to private investors
(about one-fifth of the direct loans made or one-fourth of the funds
loaned) are sold with a guaranty; in the case of default, the claim and
property acquisition costs are paid out of the loan guaranty fund.

The Housing Subsidy

In line with VA concern for the wellbeing of its clients, VA regulations afford lenders broad discretion in extending or redesigning the
terms of the loan to allow the borrower to retain his property, if he
faces default. Nonetheless, defaults do occur and the VA consequently
becomes involved in acquiring and selling property. When a guaranteed loan is foreclosed, the lender has the option of reselling the property or, as is done in most cases, of conveying it to the VA. In the case
of direct loans, the property title is conveyed directly to the VA. The
VA, in turn, normally resells its properties through local real estate
brokers, although in some instances buyers can finance the property
purchase with the VA. As of the end of fiscal 1972, over 270,000 home
loans or 3.5 percent of the 7.8 million home loans guaranteed since
1944 were foreclosed and claims paid by the VA.

The low rate of foreclosure under the VA home loan programs,
combined with similar successes in the FHA programs, have acted as a
liberalizing influence on mortgage practices. According to one authori-
tative estimate, approximately $1 billion annually in benefits accrues
to participants in these loan programs due mainly to tax savings by
the mortgagees.[33]

VA loan guarantees and direct loans are made to veterans who
meet the qualifications of sound income and satisfactory credit rating
necessary in the market for mortgage funds. The low income veteran
seeking housing assistance must turn to the FHA on the same terms as
nonveterans. Rent supplements and public housing programs are de-

signed to offer preferences to low-income families, the handicapped, and the elderly, and do not extend preferences on the basis of veteran status alone.

The VA loan program raises two issues for the study of the veterans' welfare system. First, what advantages does the VA program offer to exservicemen not available to the rest of the population? Also, to what extent is the program subsidized by the U.S. Treasury?

Federal Housing Administration (FHA) loan insurance parallels the VA home loan program. A comparison of the terms of FHA and VA loans for single-family, owner-occupied homes demonstrates the basic similarities of the two programs. Both VA guarantees and FHA insurance allow a thirty-year repayment plan on any standard amortizing schedule established by the lender. Neither loan involves a prepayment penalty. However, the VA home loan guaranty has two significant advantages. First, the FHA insures home loans up to $33,000, for which the homebuyer pays an additional one-half of one percent interest on his loan. The VA loan guaranty involves no additional interest charge over the base rate. Since 1966, the VA has been allowed to set interest rates competitive with FHA rates. Previously, the maximum allowable VA rate was set by Congress, which did not act as quickly as necessary to respond to changes in market conditions. The second advantage for the veteran is the difference in down payment under the VA and FHA programs. As long as the veteran's loan is for the reasonable value of the home established by the VA, he is not required to make a down payment, unless, of course, the lender demands one. Regular FHA standards allow loan insurance to cover 97 percent of the first $15,000 of the value of the loan, 90 percent of the next $10,000, and 80 percent of any amount over $25,000. A veteran purchasing a $30,000 home at 7 percent on a thirty year term would make no downpayment and pay $199.60 per month in principal and interest while a nonveteran buying the same home with FHA insurance would be required to make a down payment of $2,450 and would pay $204.29 monthly.[34] Thus, the veteran would save over $4,000 over the life of the mortgage. As a result of the differences in interest rates and down payments, the VA and FHA housing programs have income redistribution and transfer implications. While the $1/2$ of one percent additional charge to FHA participants redistributes income from higher-income homebuyers who are lower risks to low-income participants who are greater risks, the VA program involves no redistribution of income among participants. Instead, the VA guarantees are largely income transfers to the predominantly middle-income veterans who participate. Moreover, because VA loan guarantees are more likely to cover loans close to the full value of the home, even at higher income levels than the FHA insurance, income transfers to veterans are larger.[35]

Both the VA loan guaranty program and the direct loan program are operated from revolving funds. Although the primary goal of the VA housing program is to provide viable credit assistance to veterans, among the secondary goals is the management of financing to avoid congressional appropriations and losses to the government. Prior to 1962, the loan guaranty program was financed directly by appropriations, and receipts were deposited in the general fund of the Treasury. Appropriations for the guaranty program totalled $730 million between 1944 and 1962. A loan guaranty revolving fund was established in 1962 and as of the end of fiscal year 1972 had a net loss of $100 million. The only appropriations made since the inception of the revolving funds have been to meet shortages in the sale of participation certificates, amounting by the end of 1972 to $18.6 million. These instruments were sold when high discount rates prevented the sale of entire loans. The direct loan fund, on the other hand, which had been in operation since 1950, enjoyed a $251.3 million surplus. This fund borrows from the Treasury at its loan rate and then lends the money to veterans at a higher rate. An additional $472 million was spent on administrative expenses—a little over $50 per loan. The resulting net cost of the VA housing program at the end of fiscal year 1972 was $320.4 million. This does not include the $120.4 million paid for special adaptive housing for disabled veterans, which is also administered by the loan guaranty personnel. Considering the services performed by the VA and the benefits accruing to those veterans who participate, the costs of the home loan program have been reasonable.

Although the loan guaranty program may not appeal to Vietnam veterans immediately upon their return home, it will most likely result in considerable savings to those men who eventually settle down to a job, a family, and a home. But, unlike the federally-supported FHA program which charges a fee to homebuyers, the VA loan guaranty is free to veterans. Since the government assumes the risk without receiving compensation from the veterans, the VA loan program is another example of a publicly subsidized program whose benefits can accrue only to veterans.

Assessment

The Vietnam veterans who have drifted back into civilian life have faced a variety of social and economic problems, the most important of which have been locating jobs and embarking on renewing a program of education. Many were combat soldiers and were too young to acquire a skill or profession prior to entering service; few had learned a salable skill while in the armed forces. Since 1969 they have had to compete for jobs in a recession or high unemployment economy and the high price of education did not always make the return to school an attractive choice.

The readjustment kit provided to their predecessors from earlier wars had been refined and expanded to offer Vietnam veterans a wide range of preferences and benefits in employment and education. But despite the sustained efforts by the VA and other federal agencies' efforts to inform them of their options, many veterans were not helped by the readjustment programs. While 1972 increases in the GI bill stipends may encourage some of the job seekers to enter school or training programs, the veteran's job search will continue to be his most important readjustment problem. At the same time, employment programs for veterans remained the weakest tool in his readjustment kit.

Job creation and employment services for veterans have relied largely on rhetoric. While the public employment service maintains a priority for veterans seeking jobs, it has traditionally listed a limited number of jobs and relatively few veterans received substantial assistance through its services. President Nixon's directive to the employment service to expand job opportunities for veterans added little real help. The anticipated 1.2 million job orders from federal government contractors failed to materialize, and it is doubtful whether the National Alliance for Businessmen's much ballyhooed pledge of 100,000 jobs for veterans created a significant number of jobs except in corporate press releases.

On the other hand, priority for veterans in federal employment and job creation programs during a period of high unemployment in the economy discriminated against other disadvantaged individuals who may have required equal or greater services. Veterans who filled the public employment program's jobs during 1972 were largely white, high school graduates, and less than three of ten were disadvantaged. Establishing such priorities may have been politically expedient, but not necessarily equitable. Despite the outreach efforts undertaken by the VA to attract more GI bill trainees, no attempt was ever made to determine who the millions of veterans were who did not choose education or training assistance and what services they might require.

For veterans who chose to return to school or training, the VA is the largest single source of readjustment assistance. However, little is known about the effectiveness of the VA programs. Follow-up of GI bill trainees is nonexistent. The VA apparently considers its mandate completed once the veteran exhausts eligibility or leaves the program for any other reason. For disabled veterans, whose programs of study are more closely monitored, the agency keeps score of those rehabilitated, but does not follow up to determine whether they continue to advance in employment; all disabled veterans who complete their course of training or education are automatically counted among the "rehabilitated." It is significant, however, to stress that VA does not restrict participation in the rehabilitation program to potential success cases. On the contrary, the more disabled the veteran, the greater the interest of the VA in helping him.

In the absence of follow-up data on the impact of readjustment programs on participating veterans, no clear determination can be made whether the taxpayers' money is being invested wisely. For example, the widespread enrollment by a large proportion of veterans using GI bill benefits in correspondence courses offer room to question the effectiveness of the readjustment program. Follow-up information from GAO on those veterans who failed to complete correspondence training tended to support the speculation that those courses are a waste of the veteran's time and the public's money. Many veterans are lured into correspondence programs under false pretences and fail to learn a useful skill.

VA educational programs are inherently biased in favor of higher education. A college student receives his full-time training stipend for 14 credit hours per week, while the veteran enrolled in "below college" technical or vocational schools must attend at least 25 hours per week of training. Moreover, a college student can change his career goal several times in the course of completing his four year degree. Veterans in vocational and on-the-job training programs cannot switch their occupational objective as freely.

There is no argument that individuals should have a free choice of what types of training and education to pursue and that the VA provides the veteran such an opportunity to select his own program of study. Moreover, the GI bill is used by many to acquire a higher education that they otherwise might not have completed. According to one estimate, about one-fourth of the post-World War II college education undertaken by veterans would not have been completed without the help of the GI bill.[36] While providing those men with the chance to realize their highest potential is a worthy social goal, it raises questions regarding the desirability of providing preference to veterans in education and, within that preference, of encouraging more and more veterans to choose college-level programs. First, the government does not offer other individuals in the society equal incentives to continue their education as those offered to veterans and this conflicts with the principles of equity. The second, more crucial question, is whether the government should induce veterans to pursue programs of higher education while both society and the individual may benefit from an expansion of the supply of craftsmen and individuals with skilled trades.

CHAPTER 5

The Future of Veterans' Programs

With malice toward none; with charity for all;
with firmness in the right, as God gives us to see
the right, let us strive to finish the work we are
in; to bind up the nation's wounds; to care for
him who shall have borne the battle, and for his
widow and his orphan—to do all which may achieve
and cherish a just and lasting peace among ourselves
and with all nations.

Abraham Lincoln
Second Inaugural Address,
March 4, 1865

In the continuing debate over the scope of federal responsibility for social welfare, programs to aid veterans have been sheltered behind a broad concensus. The desirability of veterans' benefits has been unquestioned; their funding has received hardly a whisper of reproach. This broad support has endured because even the most adamant foes of federal spending recognize the nation's debt to those who served in the armed forces. Moreover, half the adult male population is potentially eligible for VA benefits, a constituency that would make far less justifiable programs politically popular.

This absence of controversy has allowed the VA to lead a tranquil and unexamined life. No coterie of critics carps at is spending, no muckraking journalists sift through its files searching for wrongdoing, and even the members of Congress and appropriations committees are happy to augment appropriations for veterans' programs. But the VA's satus as a "sacred cow" has also limited straightforward evaluation and review of the agency. It should not be unpatriotic to ask how well the billions dispensed by the VA and other federal agencies are spent.

The times are auspicious for a critical review of the national efforts on behalf of veterans. The armed forces are undergoing radical changes that bear significant implications for future programs for veterans. After more than three decades, forced conscription into the armed forces is being replaced by an all volunteer armed forces. And with termination of the unfortunate war in southeast Asia, the nation may hope for a respite from armed conflicts.

This is a good time to rethink and revamp the nation's veterans

policy. Two issues are involved: (1) how well does the VA meet its
legislated goals, and (2) are these goals still as worthy as they were
when the legislation was enacted? Given the mandates of the legislation, does the VA do a creditable job administering its programs?
Compared to other government agencies delivering similar services,
how efficient is the VA? Is the rationale which supports the various
veterans' laws as valid today as it was originally, and will it remain
valid in the future? It is important to answer these questions, at least
tentatively, before considering directions for the future.

How Effective Is the VA?

Evaluations of government programs seldom gush with praise
unless they are prepared by the officials responsible for the programs.
The VA has escaped the criticism that hounds other government efforts
because its activities are usually isolated from the scrutiny that other
government agencies face. Information about government efforts on
behalf of veterans is available only from VA sources.

Given the caveat that some skeletons may remain hidden in the
closets, the public record of the VA is surprisingly free of blemishes.
The difficulties which have been noted in the delivery of some services
are bound to be part of a large bureaucratic organization. In most
cases VA services are effectively delivered, with a maximum of respect
for the recipient and a minimum of delay from governmental intri-
cacies. Contrary to the conventional wisdom about the rigidity that
engulfs long-established bureaucratic organizations, the VA officialdom
remains unusually sensitive to the needs of its clientele.

In providing income support to the disabled and indigent, the VA
system makes every attempt within the law to see that real needs are
met. In contrast to the common welfare concept of delivering "the least
aid sufficient to sustain," the VA's philosophy might be phrased as
providing the "most generous help short of waste." Although some
argue that the VA's magnanimity has led to duplication and over-
spending, it is probable that this debit is outweighed by the greater
benefits which flow from a liberal system. The administrative costs are
cut because the presumption of "innocence" simplifies the certification
of eligibility. Most important, those to whom the programs are
directed retain their self-esteem, and escape the stigma of public charity.
Excluding the personnel that administer and operate hospitals, the
VA supplies income-support and services to millions of veterans with a
remarkably small administrative staff.

This general effectiveness of VA income support programs is not
unflawed; equity may be sacrificed because the law seeks uniformity of

administration. Compensation payments do not cover true economic loss in many cases, and the single level of payment for given degrees of disability does not consider individual and occupational variations. Pensions, too, are imperfectly designed. Though veterans' pensions are relatively generous to some, the level of benefits is too low to permit veterans with no other income to escape poverty. These drawbacks deserve legislative attention. In a broad sense, though, the government has done well by veterans in providing them income support.

The VA record is similarly impressive in its delivery of hospital care, and Congress has been willing to foot the bill. VA health care for the poor and the disabled could easily have become submarginal care inefficiently delivered to those with little voice to protest for better. But VA hospitals evidently provide above average care to large numbers at low per diem costs. The VA medical officials have taken the initiative, with congressional backing, to secure medical school ties, research grants, and expanded medical services to insure that the quality of medical care remains high. At the same time, the cost of this care has remained below that of most community hospitals. Critics challenge the VA's long average hospital stays and lenient standards for medical indigence and argue for restricted access to VA hospitals and for delivering the least care. Again, the VA philosophy is counter to this "minimum care" standard; the VA seeks instead to provide all the care that is feasible and necessary. The VA may indeed be able to cut average patient stays and eliminate service to the marginally eligible, but on its own terms, current hospital and nursing care is well delivered.

Despite some deficiencies, the VA also exerts considerable effort to insure that its services are used by those needing education and training. If employment problems persist for many recently discharged veterans, and educational opportunities are unused by many, it is less a reflection of VA efforts than of other factors. VA assistance cannot create jobs or motivate veterans to learn useful skills.

The greatest problem with the VA's provisions for educational support is that they favor college students. The higher payments to college students than to veterans pursuing skill training outside academic walls is a matter of law. But the granting to college students of broad freedom to change their educational programs and career goals, while vocational and technical students must define their career goals at the beginning of their course of study and are allowed only one "change of mind" without special consultation, reflects more administrative bias than congressional intent. Fairer treatment for those who wish to learn nonacademic skills should be adopted.

The clearest example of the VA's accomplishment has been its active attempt to bring its programs to its clients. Capitalizing on a captive military audience, and following up veterans with outreach programs which only stop short of "begging" potential recipients, the VA's policy is a singularly notable case of affirmative government action.

It is obvious that the effectiveness of most VA programs has been possible because of the stout support provided the VA by Congress and the public. Repeatedly, problems in the delivery of services have been recognized and quickly corrected by legislative and administrative changes. Pensions which drastically penalized marginal income were altered; earnings limitations on the payment of on-the-job training benefits were abolished; underutilization of programs by Vietnam veterans was countered with efforts to reach the potential clients who did not apply for VA benefits; hospitals which needed top quality medical personnel were linked to medical schools. These continuous efforts to improve veterans' programs reflect the universal agreement over goals. Shortcomings in these services need only to be pin-pointed to be corrected. Obviously this concensus has been virtually unique among government welfare programs.

The logic of this concensus deserves examination. Few doubt the success of the VA on its own terms. But are those terms still as perfectly justified as they were formerly? Do the programs meet standards of equity? The question is less how well do we serve veterans than how well *should* we serve veterans? Do they deserve better than they are getting? Do others deserve the same?

The Rationale for Veterans' Programs

Even a cursory survey of veterans' programs reveals that they are supported by two distinct rationales. Some VA benefits are compensation for individual loss. Disability payments, hospital care to the wounded, unemployment insurance, reemployment rights, and survivors' compensation are clearly attempts to recompense or minimize economic losses. Other programs, just as clearly, are not compensation but preferences granted to a special group because it is deemed more deserving. Pensions to old and disabled veterans, hospital care for nonservice-connected disabilities, employment programs, and, to some extent, education and housing subsidies are programs which seek to provide for veterans' needs simply because they served, rather than because this military service deprived them or caused their needs. The distinction between these justifications is crucial if the logic of veterans' programs is to be tested against present and evolving social standards.

Veterans' Programs as Compensation

Service to the nation during wartime involves sacrifices. Those who join the battle have certainly lost time from other pursuits, have probably lost income, and may have lost limb or life. Governmental responsibility for these losses is clearest in the case of draftees. Conscripts are forced to fight in order to implement national goals. A just government indisputably owes these men for the losses they suffer as a result of its decisions. But even when men enlist for war service, the government sill bears the responsibility for their losses. Although millions of war veterans have volunteered, it is safe to assume that had there been no national decision to wage war, these men would not have suffered the losses of war service. Even a career soldier who requests hazardous duty has not relieved the government of its responsibility for incurred losses, should he become disabled. Men volunteer for risk, but none choose to be disabled. The nation as a whole bears the responsibility for those losses.

The rationale for compensation, then, derives directly from the decision to demand that citizens serve during wartime. The debt owed to those who "fight the peace," however, it not so clearcut. Presumably, in the absence of a draft or a massive mobilization to defend the nation, those who volunteer for military service during peacetime have evidently been compensated in advance for any deprivations associated with this service in order to stimulate them to join. Voluntary service in the military during peacetime is not a special service exacted by the nation from some of its citizens, but a chosen profession receiving sufficient emoluments and benefits to make it worthwhile. The government owes its permanent military establishment the respect, security, workmen's compensation in case of injury, and pay due all public servants. But in the absence of war, it does not owe servicemen for special sacrifices.

It is important to consider this distinction as the nation closes a tragic war and strives to return to a volunteer military establishment. The maintenance of a large peacetime military force will inevitably create pressure to retain present benefits to all veterans. Discarding the original justification of providing for those who have suffered unequal loss, the veterans of peace are likely to insist that they deserve the same benefits accorded to those who have preceeded them in uniform.

The "losses" of peacetime service should in fact be pared considerably in the future. As military pay is raised to match civilian scales, the arguments for economic losses will be inapplicable. As career soldiers replace draftees, the education, retirement, and disability compensation benefits available to regular military personnel should make similar VA programs superfluous. In the absence of new wars or continuing conscription, compensation for special losses should be replaced by direct benefits paid by the military to its present and former members. Presently VA and military hospitals serve retired and disabled career servicemen who are eligible for either VA or military disability compensation and survivors' benefits. The VA, an agency created to recompense those who were temporarily called to serve, should not continue to be required to care for those who make the military a career.

VA Programs as Preferential Welfare

Not all veterans' programs can be justified as compensation for service-generated needs. Only by great leaps of the imagination can the impoverishment of older nondisabled veterans be traced to their war-time service. Similarly, hospital care to the nonservice disabled is by definition unrelated to military deprivations. Although educational benefits are extended to all veterans in part because they were subjected not only to a disruption in their lives but also economic hardship and postponement of their careers, it is doubtful that the GI bill is really justified as compensation. The evidence indicates that veterans, rather than suffering economic hardship, eventually earn *more* than their nonveteran counterparts. Although some case can be made for the greater difficulties of going to school at 21 than at 18, surely the older men do not need an extra $8,000 to put them on an equal footing with those who did not serve.

An even more obvious case is the housing subsidy to veterans. This benefit is rarely exercised until several years after service is completed, by which time veterans as a group are more affluent than nonveterans. It seems questionable indeed to justify this program as a compensatory measure.

Clearly these programs, whatever their original rationale, are supported now because they benefit a group of citizens deemed deserving of help. It is, of course, society's right to designate favorites for its largesse, and veterans, by any estimate, rank high among those whose service merits thanks.

On the other hand, the thrust of most of the social welfare legislation of the past two decades has been redistribution based on need rather than some criterion of merit. When veterans' programs for the needy were initiated, they were the only welfare programs available. The law-makers agreed to single out for support poor veterans and their widows because they were "deserving." Since that time new programs for the population at large have been enacted, as government and the public have assumed broader social responsibilities. It is accepted, albeit sometimes reluctantly, that all who are sick deserve medical care and that even the poor deserve to eat and to be sheltered. This evolution of the nation's social conscience erodes the justification of special treatment granted to veterans who have suffered no loss from military service.

Programs for veterans have been path-breakers in the evolution of legislated social welfare. But this role of pioneering social legislation has been transformed by the development of broad welfare coverage. Veterans' programs have ceased to be the only public aid to the needy, but have become instead supplemental and superior public aid. The powerful constituency which supports veterans' legislation has consistently persuaded Congress that veterans deserve better, no matter what provisions are made for others.

The social security and public assistance laws, which were designed to provide minimum income support to the old and disabled, have in theory obviated the need for separate veterans' programs. But instead of withering away, pensions continued to grow. As benefits under social security were raised, eligibility for pensions kept pace, assuring not only that veterans' pensions would not be reduced as a result of rising social insurance benefits, but qualifying others who may not have been eligible under earlier lower income ceilings. For example, when Congress raised in 1969 Old Age and Survivors Benefits by 15 percent, it soon adjusted veterans' pensions to assure that the higher social security benefits did not displace veterans from pension rolls or cause pensioners to loose any part of their benefits. If this trend is not to be arrested, then the number of veterans and survivor pensioners are likely to more than double during the next two decades. Possibly, the 1972 boost in social security benefits of 20 percent may be the Rubicon for the trend of future pensions. As in the past, bills were introduced in Congress that would have raised income eligibility and exemptions preventing a reduction in pension payments. In 1972, however, the House followed Veterans Committee Chairman Olin E. Teague's recommendation and did not raise pension income limits. As a result, the higher social security income exceeded the ceiling of pension eligibility, and 20,000 veterans were scheduled to loose their pensions. But it is premature to equate this brief flurry of congressional resistance with a lasting change of policy. With powerful advocates in Congress and an influential lobby it would be surprising if legislation upping pension income limits failed to be enacted.

Veterans' health care has been even less affected by new government programs for expanded health care to the aged and indigent. Since VA hospitals are free and less demeaning than alternative government medical plans, the continuing popularity of veterans' health care is not hard to understand. Although Medicare and Medicaid initially decreased VA hospital use, seven years after the passage of these programs Congress voted the highest ever annual appropriation for construction and expansion of VA health facilities. Even with powerful presidential support, efforts to trim these health care outlays have always been defeated in the past and it is unlikely that veterans' health care outlays will be cut back in the near future. President Lyndon Johnson did try to cut appropriations for the building of VA hospitals. He lost the battle and President Richard Nixon took the cue and never fought to cut VA hospital appropriations.

Congressman John T. Saylor of Pennsylvania later recalled the incident:

> We took it right to the floor and we whipped him. Then we whipped him again the next year and when we whipped him the third time he finally came to us and said, "All right, I surrender, how much do you want?

Congressman Saylor, a Republican, then warned the Nixon administration:

> We are going to do the same thing for . . . the present Administration, we are going to get . . . the amount of money which . . . you require . . . for medical care.[1]

Because of this steady expansion, and despite availability of alternative coverage, preferential programs now account for the largest portion of outlays for veterans' compensation. Service payments account for about one-fourth of total expenditures. Only one in six VA hospital patients is receiving treatment for a service disability. Unemployment insurance has added little to the total compensatory payments.

If Congress continues to sweeten these preferential programs, VA outlays may swell substantially. Although readjustment benefits should fall as the Vietnam war is terminated and military manpower stabilizes, some of these benefits are of long duration. Housing subsidies have no time limits on their use, and educational stipends may be utilized for eight years after separation from the military. Future pensions may be still more costly. By 1990 as many as 5.7 million veterans and their surviving dependents may be receiving pensions if income limits are kept above social security benefit levels. Moreover, expenditures for VA medical care will also continue to expand if present trends continue and VA care remains so clearly superior to other forms of government-supported health care. Thus only readjustment allowances are likely to decline in the years ahead, and this assumes that the war in Southeast Asia was our last war. Hope springs eternal, but the dream of turning swords into plowshares is not a discovery of the space age and the experience in the twentieth century hardly justifies excessive optimism on this score.

The fact that veterans' benefits will probably continue to rise in the future, perhaps dramatically, does not necessarily argue for their reduction or elimination. Obviously pensions which still do not raise the poorest above the poverty line should be increased, not curtailed, unless an alternative source for income support is provided. The health care for veterans can be counted as wasteful only by those who claim the hospitals are filled with malingerers. And the benefits provided by education and housing subsidies can be questioned as unneeded only by the most fiscally conservative.

But the recognition that these programs are clearly preferential in an era in which public policy has nominally sought greater equity and general welfare for all suggests that some reevaluation may be called for. Do all indigent veterans deserve higher incomes than the neediest nonveterans? Do only veterans deserve financial help in obtaining an education, or should the most educationally disadvantaged be given greater priority? Should employers be encouraged to hire and train veterans over nonveterans? Should veterans, who generally have higher incomes, receive housing loan guarantees, or should these subsidies be granted to all? Should free, accessible, undemeaning medical care be reserved for veterans or is dignity and good health the equal right of all?

Future Directions

It would be harsh, as well as politically naive, to suggest that veterans' programs should be cut back to levels identical with other welfare programs. But it should not be amiss to suggest that public policy in the future be directed toward bringing universal welfare programs up to the VA standards. Veterans have been the sirens who were able to call forth government support for their needs. The VA, whose design and administration of welfare programs have been exemplary, might become the precursor of and the model for a liberal, humane, and respected welfare system for all. A careful review of the VA experience suggests lessons that can be gleaned from the veterans' programs which would be useful to help restructure and improve the nation's welfare system.

The problem which has plagued programs for social welfare seems deceptively simple: how do you give away money and services to those with the most need without impeding efforts for self-help? How does the government efficiently distribute help to specific groups in a

way which both respects the recipients and also insures that the aid
goes to those for whom it was intended?

The VA has been dealing with these problems longer than any
other agency. Its experience should not be ignored in the debate over
revamping the welfare system.

1. Having rejected a universal income support program, Congress
may wisely adopt the VA's simple, liberal means test, relying on
recipients' honesty, in lieu of the demeaning barriers and examinations erected by states around other welfare programs. The VA system cuts administrative overhead because no laborious rechecking is
done to weed out "chiselers." Although this method certainly
allows some to receive benefits who should not, its basic effect is
simply to liberalize eligibility criteria. Horrendous anecdotes not-
withstanding, it is doubtful that many well-to-do apply for VA
pensions or hospital care because this relatively minimum help is
obtainable by lying. If some of the marginally eligible receive benefits by misrepresenting their status, these added costs are justified by
the general gain to recipients' self-esteem which a system built on
mutual respect engenders. This kind of shared dignity must be the
foundation of any humane welfare system. In brief, based on the
VA experience, Congress could act to take the meanness out of the
means test.

2. VA outreach efforts could be the model for government action
to find and enlist potential recipients for help. If society decides
that it has a responsibility to help some of its members, then it
should not only make that help available, but actively seek to deliver
it. The VA has never forced its programs on the unwilling, but in
recent years it has persistently sought to insure that none fail to
receive benefits because they are uninformed of their rights, or because the bureaucracy is too complex or imposing. The VA adopted
the ombudsman approach long before the antipoverty warriors popu-
larized the term. This example deserves emulation.

3. VA health care could be considered as a more efficient alternative to the vendor payment system for government subsidy of medical care. The VA has demonstrated it can deliver above average care
at below average cost. Health care to the needy so delivered is easier
to obtain, less demeaning, and socially less costly than Medicare or
Medicaid. If the nation is truly committed to caring for all who
need medical attention, then it should evaluate the VA hospital
system carefully and draw from it. If overutilization problems can
be solved, VA health care might deserve to become the model and
the backbone of a national health care system.

4. The VA experience in refining its pension payment system
could be adopted to the welfare system to eliminate the "notch"

problem, and insure that the most aid goes to the most needy. The VA's system of gradually lowered payments preserves the incentive to work and eases the hardship of exceeding the income ceiling. This method, further improved, should be utilized in other welfare programs.

If the nation moves in the direction indicated, then consideration should be given to focusing VA activity on compensation and care for those who have suffered loss in war. The VA's preferential welfare programs might consequently be gradually melded with programs for the whole population.

The VA has inexorably tended to expand its functions and almost everyone has supported it. Though it has executed these responsibilities well, it has grown beyond its legitimate compensatory role.

Rather than concentrating on the preferred class of veterans, socially just programs should aim to help the most needy first and should seek eventually to raise all above minimum standards. The separate pension system could be maintained until universal income support reaches comparable levels, and then could wither away. VA hospitals, on the other hand, might better be integrated into a national health care system by expanding hospital facilities and opening the doors to all needy. If the government decides to subsidize education, such aid should be granted not only to veterans, but to all needy students. The VA certification and stipend system could, with some refinements, be adapted to serve all those aspiring to a college education or to skill training but who lack the means to achieve their goals. But considering the costs, a selective process will have to be designed to limit outlays within acceptable bounds. On the other hand, VA housing subsidies have stimulated the housing market and saved homeowners billions of dollars at a minimal cost to the government. Such enormous benefits accruing at so little cost could easily be extended to others.

Whether the unification of these separate and unequal welfare systems takes place within the framework of the existing VA structure or whether VA programs are gradually supplanted and absorbed into a universal system is not important. But, in time, aid to needy veterans should be replaced by aid to needy citizens.

The suggested policy considerations may seem heretical to supporters of the status quo. But in view of the recent rapid expansion of the welfare system, the indicated future direction of veterans' programs may be at hand. President Nixon has already proposed a minimum guaranteed income for all, and Congress may adopt the approach before too long. If a guaranteed, albeit, minimal income becomes a reality, much of the need for a separate veterans' pension system will diminish. Similarly, the adoption of a national health program would

obviate the need for a separate veteran hospital system. Since half of
the adult male population consists of veterans, the continuation of two
welfare systems may become untenable.

No one doubts the justice of programs to care for those who have
suffered and sacrificed in defense of the country. Nor do many challenge the VA's commendable record in delivering this care and other
benefits. But a nation dedicated to justice for all should care for all its
needy before it gives special favors to those who have suffered no loss
even if they have served.

Notes

Chapter 1

1. Quoted by Robinson E. Adkins, *Medical Care of Veterans* (Washington: Government Printing Office, 1967), p. 21.

2. *Ibid.*, p. 29.

3. Richard Hofstadter, William Miller, and Daniel Aaron, *The United States: The History of a Republic* (Englewood Cliffs, N.J.: Prentice Hall, 1957), p. 141–42.

4. Adkins, *Medical Care of Veterans*, p. 30.

5. President's Commission on Veterans' Pensions, *A Report on Veterans' Benefits in the United States: Findings and Recommendations* (Washington: Government Printing Office, 1956), pp. 3–4.

6. U.S. Congress, Committee on Veterans' Affairs, *The Administration of Veterans' Benefits*, A Report on Veterans' Benefits in the United States by the President's Commission on Veterans' Pensions, Staff Report VI, June 19, 1956, 84th Cong., 2nd sess., p. 10.

7. Lynch v. United States, 292 U.S. 571.

8. William H. Harader, *The Committee on Veterans Affairs: A Study of the Legislative Process and Milieu As They Pertain to Veterans Legislation* (Ann Arbor, Mich.: University Microfilms, Inc., 1968), pp. 28, 30.

9. Arnold Bortz, "American Legion's Influence Wanes on Capitol Hill," *National Journal*, June 8, 1970, p. 1313.

10. P. F. Kluge, "Bygone Battles," *The Wall Street Journal*, May 19, 1971, p. 1.

11. Unpublished letter from Robert B. Pitkin, editor of the *American Legion Magazine* to Warren H. Phillips of *The Wall Street Journal*, May 24, 1971.

12. *Congressional Record* (daily edition), August 6, 1972, p. E9143.

13. Interview with Francis W. Stover, director, National Legislative Service, Veterans of Foreign Wars, April 3, 1972.

14. U.S. Congress, Senate Committee on Appropriations, *Department of Housing and Urban Development; Space, Science, Veterans and Certain Other Independent Agencies Appropriations, Fiscal Year 1972*, 92nd Cong., 1st sess., 1971, p. 542.

15. U.S. Congress, House Committee on Appropriations, *Hearings, HUD-Space-Science Appropriations for 1972*, 92nd Cong., 2nd sess., 1971, pp. 82, 83.

16. Testimony of Senator Alan Cranston, Senate Committee on Appropriations, *Department of Housing and Urban Development; Space, Science, Veterans and Certain Ohter Independent Agencies Appropriations*, p. 629.

17. U.S. Congress, Senate Committee on Veterans' Affairs, *A Study of the Problems Facing Vietnam Era Veterans on Their Readjustment to Civilian Life*, by *Louis Harris and Associates, Inc.*, Senate Committee Print No. 7, 92nd Cong., 2nd sess., January 31, 1972, pp. 239, 247.

Chapter 2

1. *Congress and the Nation: 1945–1964, A Review of Government Policies* (Washington: Congressional Quarterly Services, 1965), 1:1349.

2. U.S. Congress, House Committee on Veterans Affairs, House Doc. no. 109, *Economic Validation of the Rating Schedule*, 92nd Cong., 1st sess., 1971, p. 18.

3. U.S. Department of Labor, *State Workmen's Compensation Laws: A Comparison of Major Professions with Recommended Standards*, Bulletin 212, 1971, p. 31.

4. U.S. Department of Labor, Employment Standards Administration, unpublished tables, "Maximum and Minimum Benefits for Permanent Total Disability" and "Maximum and Minimum Benefits for Permanent Partial Disability," January 1, 1972.

5. U.S. Department of Defense, "Number of Military Receiving Retired Pay at the End of Fiscal Years 1971–1973, and Total Amount of Retired Pay Disbursements."

6. William Glasson, *Federal Military Pensions in the United States* (New York: Oxford University Press, 1918), p. 91.

7. U.S. Congress, House Committee on Veterans Affairs, Subcommittee on Compensation and Pensions, *Pending Pension and Dependency/Indemnity Compensation Bills,* testimony of Olney B. Owen, chief benefits director, Veterans Administration, 92nd Cong., 1st sess., 1971, p. 1257.

8. U.S. Department of Labor, Office of Information, USDL 72–856, January 2, 1973.

9. U.S. Congress, House Committee on Veterans Affairs, *Review of VA Insurance Programs,* 92nd Cong., 1st sess., 1971, p. 840.

10. Warren H. MacDonald, "What Should Constitute Need for Purposes of Entitlement to Veterans Disability Pension," mimeographed paper, 1959, p. 14.

11. Gilbert Y. Steiner, *The State of Welfare* (Washington: The Brookings Institution, 1971), p. 245.

12. U.S. Congress, House Committee on Veterans Affairs, Subcommittee on Compensation and Pensions, *Pending Pension and Dependency/Indemnity Compensation Bills,* 92d Cong., 1st sess., 1971, p. 983.

13. U.S. General Accounting Office, *Need for Improved Procedures to Minimize Overpayments of Non-Service-Connected Disability and Death Pensions,* GAO Report no. B–114859 (December 28, 1967), p. 4.

14. U.S. Congress, House Subcommittee on Appropriations, *HUD-Space-Science-Veterans Appropriations for 1973,* 92nd Cong., 2nd sess., 1972, p. 674.

15. President's Commission on Veterans' Pensions, *A Report on Veterans' Benefits in the United States: Findings and Recommendations* (Washington: Government Printing Office, 1956), p. 138.

16. U.S. Congress, House Committee on Veterans Affairs, Subcommittee on Compensation and Pensions, *Bills to Increase Compensation Rates and to Increase Pension Limitations and Rates,* 92nd Cong., 2nd sess., 1970, p. 2756.

17. U.S. Veterans Administration, Department of Veterans Benefits, *1971 Long Range Trends,* January 1971.

Chapter 3

1. U.S. Veterans Administration, "VA Organizational Manual," change 202, August 18, 1972, p. II–2.

2. U.S. Congress, House Subcommittee on Appropriations, *HUD-Space-Sceince Appropriations for 1971,* 92nd Cong., 1st sess., 1971, p. 87.

3. U.S. Code, Title 38, chapter 17, sec. 610.

4. U.S. Veterans Administration, unpublished report, "Racial Breakdown for VA Beneficiaries Remaining in and Discharged from VA Hospitals—1971–1972," Office of the Controller, September 11, 1972.

5. U.S. Congress, House Veterans Committee, *Operations of the Veterans Administration Hospital and Medical Program,* 92nd Cong., 1st sess., 1971, pp. 84–85.

6. *Ibid.,* p. 7.

7. Robinson E. Adkins, *Medical Care of Veterans* (Washington: Government Printing Office, 1967), appendix B, pp. 395–409.

8. Paul B. Magnuson, *Ring the Night Bell: The Autobiography of a Surgeon* (Boston: Little, Brown and Co., 1960), p. 268.

9. U.S. Congress, House Committee on Veterans Affairs, *Operations and Funding of the VA Medical Programs and Legislation Relating Thereto,* 92nd Cong., 1st sess., 1971, p. 232; and The Carnegie Commission on Higher Education, *Higher Education and the Nation's Health: Policies for Medical and Dental Education* (New York: McGraw-Hill Book Co., 1970), pp. 107–109.

10. U.S. Congress, House Committee on Veterans Affairs, *Operations of Veterans Administration Hospital and Medical Programs,* committee print no. 1, 92nd Cong., 1st sess., 1971, p. 92.

11. U.S. Department of Health, Education, and Welfare, *Health Resources Statistics: 1970* (Washington: Government Printing Office, 1971), p. 261; and American Hospital Association, *Hospitals, Guide Issue*, August 1, 1971, p. 46.

12. U.S. Veterans Administration, *Congressional Submission, Medical and Construction Appropriations and Funds*, vol. 3, fiscal year 1973, pp. 2–72.

13. U.S. Veterans Administration, *1971 Annual Report*, p. 28.

14. Herbert E. Klarman, "Increased Cost of Hospital Care," in *The Economics of Health and Medical Care: Proceedings of the Conference on the Economics of Health and Medical Care, May 10–12, 1962* (Ann Arbor: University of Michigan Press, 1964), p. 237.

15. John A. D. Cooper, quoted in "Caring for the Veterans, Will the VA Meet the Challenge," *Medical World News*, August 6, 1971, p. 3.

16. U.S. Veterans Administration, *The Future of the VA Medical Program: 1970–1990* (Washington: Veterans Administration, March 1970), p. 47.

17. Adkins, *Medical Care*, p. 62.

18. U.S. Veterans Administration, *Federal Benefits . . . for Veterans and Dependents*, Fact Sheet 1S-1 (Washington: Government Printing Office, 1971), p. 4.

19. U.S. Veterans Administration, *Veterans in Domiciliaries: A Profile Study* (Washington: Government Printing Office, 1961), pp. 1–42.

20. Leo Rosenburg, "New Concepts in Management and Care of Domiciliary Members," *Journal of the Association for Physical and Mental Rehabilitation*, 1966, p. 101.

21. U.S. Congress, House Subcommittee on Appropriations, *HUD-Space-Science Appropriations for 1972*, 92nd Cong., 1st sess., 1971, p. 424.

22. Veterans Administration, "Extended Care Service: Report of Conference . . . Hospital Based Home Care" (Washington: Veterans Administration, April 29–30, 1969), p. 1.

23. S. C. Kaim, M.D., "VA Alcoholism Programs," Veterans Administration mimeographed paper, 1971.

24. U.S. General Accounting Office, *Drug Abuse Control Program Activities in Vietnam*, GAO publication no. B–164031 (2) (August 11, 1972), pp. 1–2.

25. U.S. Congress, Senate Committee on Veterans Affairs, *A Study of the Problems Facing Vietnam Era Veterans on Their Readjustment to Civilian Life*, by Louis Harris and Associates, Inc., Senate committee print no. 7, 92nd Cong., 2nd sess., January 31, 1972, pp. 169–70.

26. Mary Russell, "Drug Therapy Aid for Vets Expanded," *The Washington Post*, June 15, 1972.

27. U.S. General Accounting Office, *Drug Abuse Control Activities Affecting Military Personnel*, GAO Report no. B–164031 (2) (August 11, 1972), pp. 20, 30, 40–41.

28. U.S. Congress, House Committee on Veterans Affairs, *Veterans' Administration Drug Dependence Program*, 92nd Cong., 2nd sess., June 1972, p. 1.

29. U.S. Congress, Senate Committee on Veterans Affairs, *Drug Addiction and Abuse Among Military Veterans*, 92nd Cong., 1st sess., 1971, pp. 135, 173.

30. American Hospital Association, *Hospital Statistics, 1971* (Chicago: American Hospital Association, 1972), p. 7; U.S. Congress, House Subcommittee on Appropriations, *HUD-Space-Science-Veterans Appropriations for 1973*, 92nd Cong., 2nd sess., 1972, p. 617; and U.S. Veterans Administration, Congressional Submission, *Medical and Construction Appropriations and Funds*, vol. 3, fiscal year 1973, sec. 2, p. 14.

31. Health Insurance Institute, *Source Book of Health Insurance Data* (New York: The Institute, 1970), p. 48.

32. Howard West, "Five Years of Medicare," *Social Security Bulletin*, December 1971, pp. 21–23.

33. Walter J. McNearny *et al.*, *Hospitals and Medical Economics: A Study of Population, Services, Costs, Methods of Payment and Controls* (Chicago: Hospital Research and Education Trust, 1962), p. 1040.

34. U.S. Congress, House Committee on Veterans Affairs, *Veterans Medical Care Act of 1971*, report no. 92–515, 92nd Cong., 1st sess., 1971, p. 2.

Chapter 4

1. National Advisory Council on Vocational Education, *Employment Problems of the Vietnam Veteran* (Washington: The Council, February 1, 1972), pp. 1, 3.

2. U.S. Veterans Administration, Reports and Statistics Service, *Data on Vietnam Era Veterans*, June 1972, p. 19.

3. Eli S. Flyer, "Profile of DOD First-Term Enlisted Personnel Separating from Active Service During 1970," *Manpower Research Note*, Office of the Assistant Secretary of Defense, October 1971, table 1; and Elizabeth Waldman, "Viet Nam War Veterans—Transition to Civilian Life," *Monthly Labor Review*, November 1970, p. 29.

4. U.S. Congress, Senate Committee on Labor and Public Welfare, Subcommittee on Veterans' Affairs, *Hearings on Unemployment and Overall Readjustment Problems of Returning Veterans*, 91st Cong., 2nd sess., December 3, 1970, p. 159.

5. U.S. Congress, Senate Committee on Veterans' Affairs, *A Study of the Problems Facing Vietnam Veterans on Their Readjustment to Civilian Life*, by Louis Harris and Associates, Inc., Senate Committee Print No. 7, 92nd Cong., 2nd sess., January 31, 1972, pp. 80–85.

6. Robert B. Richardson, *An Examination of the Transferability of Certain Military Skills and Experience to Civilian Occupations*, A Final Report of Research under Doctoral Dissertation Grant No. 91–34–66–47, U.S. Department of Labor, Office of Manpower Policy, Evaluation and Research, September 1967, pp. 16–17.

7. Paul A. Weinstein, *Labor Market Activity of Veterans: Some Aspects of Military Spillover*, Final Report of the Military Training Study to the U.S. Department of Health, Education and Welfare, Office of Education, August 1969, pp. 13–14.

8. Richardson, *Examination of the Transferability of Certain Military Skills*, p. 16.

9. Weinstein, *Labor Market Activity*, pp. 143–44.

10. U.S. Department of Defense, *Transition Program*, mimeographed paper, March 20, 1972, pp. 2–3.

11. U.S. Congress, House Committee on Veterans Affairs, *Hearings on Education and Training Programs Administered by VA*; 92nd Cong., 1st sess., November 30, 1971, pp. 1733–34.

12. Kenneth B. Hoyt, "Career Education and Career Choice: Implications for the VA," address to the Veterans Administration National Task Force on Education and the Vietnam Era Veteran, Washington, D.C., February 8, 1972, p. 10.

13. U.S. Veterans Administration, *Two Years of Outreach, 1968–1970* (Washington: Government Printing Office, 1970), p. 4.

14. U.S. Congress, Senate Committee on Veterans' Affairs, *Study of the Problems Facing Vietnam Veterans*, pp. 226–34.

15. U.S. Congress, Senate Committee on Veterans' Affairs, *Study of the Problems Facing Vietnam Veterans*, p. 78.

16. U.S. Department of Labor, Labor-Management Services Administration, *Veterans' Reemployment Rights Handbook* (Washington: Government Printing Office, 1970), pp. 1–14, 71–82.

17. U.S. Department of Labor, Veterans Employment Service, *Review and Analysis Report, The President's Veterans Program*, mimeographed report, March 31, 1972, p. 26.

18. Elizabeth Waldman and Kathryn R. Gover, "Employment Situation of Vietnam Era Veterans," *Monthly Labor Review*, September 1971, p. 7.

19. Leonard P. Adams, *The Public Employment Service in Transition, 1933–1968* (Ithaca, N.Y.: Cornell University Press, 1969), p. 43.

20. U.S. Department of Labor, "Listing of Job Vacancies with the Federal-State Employment System," *Federal Register*, September 14, 1971, pp. 18398–18400.

21. U.S. General Accounting Office, *Most Veterans Not Completing Correspondence Courses*, GAO publication no. B–114859 (March 22, 1972), pp. 8–9.

22. *Congressional Record* (daily edition), August 3, 1972, p. S12648.

23. U.S. Department of Labor, Manpower Administration, *The National Apprenticeship Program* (Washington: Government Printing Office, 1968), p. 6.

24. U.S. Bureau of the Census, *Statistical Abstract of the United States 1971* (Washington: Government Printing Office, 1972), table 196, p. 126.

25. *Statement of Sidney P. Marland, Jr., Commissioner of Education*, before the Committee on Veterans' Affairs, United States Senate, mimeographed paper, April 28, 1972.

26. Kenneth B. Hoyt, "Career Education and Career Choice: Implications for the VA," pp. 12–13.

27. "Establishment of Absolute Preference for Enrollment for Vietnam Veterans in Manpower Training Programs," Manpower Administration Order no. 3–72, March 21, 1972.

28. U.S. Congress, House Committee on Veterans' Affairs, *The Historical Development of Veterans' Benefits in the United States*, A Report on Veterans' Benefits in the United States by the President's Commission on Veterans' Pensions, Staff Report I, May 6, 1956, 84th Cong., 2nd sess., 1956, pp. 130–31.

29. U.S. Congress, House Committee on Veterans' Affairs, *Record and Evaluation of the Vocational Rehabilitation Program for Service-Connected Disabled Veterans by the Veterans Administration*, July 8, 1955, House Committee Print 109, 84th Cong., 1st sess., 1955, p. 9.

30. U.S. Veterans Administration, "Chapter 31 Programs of Study of Peacetime Disabled Veterans Cumulative by Classification of Training From January 1963 through November 30, 1970," mimeographed.

31. U.S. Veterans Administration, *Rehabilitation Rates—Vocational Rehabilitation Trainees*, unpublished table. The figures include those World War II and Korean Conflict veterans who entered training through June 30, 1971.

32. U.S. Bureau of the Census, *Statistical Abstract of the United States 1972* (Washington: Government Printing Office, 1972), p. 693.

33. Henry J. Aaron, *Shelter and Subsidies* (Washington: The Brookings Institution, 1972), pp. 84–85, 89.

34. William S. Mussenden, ed., *The Homeowner's Guide* (Washington: The Homeowner's Guide, Inc., 1971), pp. 23–27.

35. Aaron, *Shelter and Subsidies*, pp. 88–89.

36. Thrainn Eggertsson, *Economic Aspects of Higher Education Taken Under The World War II GI Bill of Rights* (Columbus, Ohio: Ohio State University Research Foundation, 1972), p. 145.

Chapter 5

1. U.S. Congress, House Committee on Veterans Affairs, *Hearings on Fundings of VA Medical Programs in 1971*, 92nd Cong., 1st sess., 1971, pp. 628–29.

List of Charts

List of Figures

List of Tables

Index

A

Accreditation, 132
Adkins, Robinson E., 8
Advance payment, 138
Age: trainees, 141; veterans, 4; Vietnam veterans, 106–9
Aid to Families with Dependent Children, 61
Aid to the Totally and Permanently Disabled, 61
Alcoholism, problem and treatment, 91–92
Allowances: on-the-job training, 139–40; subsistence, World War II, 153; training, Korean conflict, 139; training, Vietnam war, 128; training, World War II, 136; uniform, 136; vocational rehabilitation, 149
Amendments: to 1966 GI Bill, 131; to the Social Security Act, 57, 169
American Legion, 15, 18–19, 25
American Legion Magazine, 20
American Red Cross, 25
American Veterans Committee, 18, 20
AMVETS, 15
Apprenticeship: benefits, 139; participation and standards, 135; programs, 126; programs sponsored by the Labor Department, 144–46
Appropriations for veterans programs, 23–25
Approval standards, for education and training programs, 127
"Attorneys in fact," 25

B

Benefits: apprenticeship, 139; comparison of duration, World War II and Korean conflict, 137; disabled veterans, 149; duration, 137; education and training, 124, 135–36; on-the-job, 139–40; readjustment for disabled veterans, 151–52; unemployment compensation, 11, 119–20; vocational rehabilitation subsistence, 149–50
Board of Veterans Appeals, 14
"Bonus payments," 119

Bradley Commission Report, 55, 59
Bradley, General Omar N., 10, 55

C

Carnegie Commission Report on Higher Education and the Nation's Health, 78
Catholic War Veterans, 18
Characteristics: domiciled veterans, 83; trainees, 141, 144; veteran pensioners, 48–49; vocational rehabilitation enrollees, 150
Civil War veterans, 83
"Cold war" era, 12
College: compared with on-the-job and vocational training, 144; level of courses, 128; participation rate, 128–29; programs, 125–29; tuition, 136–37
Compensation for service-disabled veterans: additional payments for dependents, 35; additional statutory awards, 34; adequacy, 36–37; comparison of VA and other (federal employees, longshoremen, etc.) compensation programs, 38–40; goal, 30–31, 167; maximum monthly payment, 34; projections, 63–64; range of payments, 32–34; termination, 32; VA outlays, 29–30
Comprehensive Health Manpower Act of 1969, 82
Confederate forces, 9
Congressional support of VA programs, 22–25, 168–71
Continental Congress, 7
Cooper, Dr. John A., 81
Corcoran, John J., 20
Correspondence courses, 131–32
Cost: correspondence courses, 132; dental care, 87–88; education and training programs after World War II, 125; home loan program, 159; medical care, 70; medical education and research, 80; outpatient care, 87; residential medical care, 83; training, 140; training of disabled veterans, 153; treatment of drug-dependent veterans, 93
Counseling: disabled veterans, 148; veterans, 27–28, 117–18
Cranston, Alan, 25

D

"Dean's Committee," 80

Decentralization: of delivery system, 13–14; of services, 14

Dental care, 88–89; cost of, 87, 88, 89; demand for, 88

Department of Medicine and Surgery, 12, 69; expenditures for health care, 70–71; personnel, 69–70; program administration, 73; program justification, 69, 70–72

Dependency and Indemnity Compensation Act of 1969, 42

Disability, degree of, 31–32, 35

Disability rating schedule, 31–32

Disabled American Veterans, 13, 15, 25

Disabled veterans: benefits, 149–50, 154; compensation, 29–37; cost of training, 153; counseling, 148; eligibility, 35, 147; homebound training, 152; "Hometown Medical Program," 88; hospital care, 69, 73–74; income, compared with nondisabled, 36–38; intake and outreach, 148; outpatient care, 88; readjustment benefits, 149–50, 154; revolving loan fund, 154; special services, 152; training, 150–51; vocational rehabilitation, 147–48

Disadvantaged veterans: education, 131; "free entitlement," 131, 140

Direct loan, 157

Domiciliary care, 69, 79; clientele, 83–84; cost, 83; eligibility, 83; facilities, 84

Dorn, William Jennings Bryan, 19

Down payment, 158

Drug addiction, 92–93, 106

Drug Dependence Treatment Centers, 93

E

Economic Opportunity Act, 145

Educational attainment: veterans, 6; Vietnam veterans, 107–8

Educational programs, 11, 124 (see also Training programs); administration, 125–26; comparison of college and vocational courses, 143–44; eligibility of veterans and institutions, 126–28; loans and grants, 137–38; for nonveterans in VA hospitals, 80–82; for survivors, 44; types, 125–26, 133, 134

Education and Rehabilitation Service, 125–26

Education benefits: cost to government, 114, 125, 141; for disabled veterans, 149–50; refunds for correspondence courses, 132–33; for survivors, 44; for Vietnam veterans, 125, 128, 135–36

Education Professions Development Act, 137

Eligibility: domiciliary care, 83; hospital treatment, service-connected, 73–74, and nonservice-connected, 75; public assistance, 60–61; social security, 56–57; survivors' compensation, 41–43; survivors' pensions, 52–53; veterans' pensions, 46–47, 49–50, 61, 79; vocational rehabilitation, 35, 147

Elizabethan Poor Law, 1

Employment Service, U.S., 123–24

Executive Order 11598, 124

Exemption programs, military, 93

Expenditures for veterans: all benefits, 1–3; compensation, 29–30; correspondence courses, 132; life insurance, 45–46; medical care, 70; pensions, 29–30, 52; projections for compensation and pensions, 62–64; readjustment benefits, 114; survivors' compensation, 41; survivors' educational benefits, 44

Ex-Servicemen's Unemployment Compensation Act of 1958, 119

Extent of guaranty, 155

F

Farmers Home Administration, U.S. Department of Agriculture, 156

Farm programs, 133–34; courses for disabled veterans, 150; loan guaranty, 156

Federal assumption of veterans programs, 7–8

Federal Employment Compensation Act, 43

Federal Housing Administration, 156, 158; comparison with VA, 158

"Fifty-two Twenty Club," 119

Flight training, 134

Freedom of choice, 126, 161

Free educational entitlement, 131, 140

G

General Accounting Office: study of correspondence courses, 132; study of drug addiction, 92–93; study of pension income reporting, 51–52

GI Bill. See Legislation

Government jobs, veterans in, 122–23

Grand Army of the Republic, 15

THE JOHNS HOPKINS UNIVERSITY PRESS

This book was composed in Baskerville text and Baskerville
display type by Monotype Composition Company. It was
printed on S. D. Warren's 60-lb. Sebago, regular finish,
text color by Universal Lithographers, Inc., and bound
in Holliston Roxite.

Library of Congress Cataloging in Publication Data

Levitan, Sar A

  Old wars remain unfinished.
  Includes bibliographical references.
    1. Veterans—United States. I. Cleary, Karen A.,
joint author. II. Title.

UB357 L47   362.8   73-8117
ISBN 0-8018-1515-0